Food ar
Spain

AA Publishing

A Spanish farmer carefully tends his vines, which are growing on a raised, stony terrace.

Original text by Pepita Aris
New text and updates by Camilo Bosso Cox

Produced by AA Publishing
© Automobile Association Developments Limited 2008
Map © Automobile Association Developments Limited 2008
Updated 2008

A CIP catalogue record for this book is available from the British Library.

ISBN 978-0-7495-5949-6

A03675

Published by AA Publishing, a trading name of Automobile Association Developments Limited, whose registered office is Fanum House, Basing View, Basingstoke, Hampshire RG21 4EA. Registered number 1878835.

Colour separation by Keenes, Andover, UK
Printed and bound in China by Everbest

Contents

About this Book

One of the pleasures of travelling is sampling the local food and drink. Whether your tastes are adventurous or conservative, this book will whet your appetite and give you a genuine taste of Spain. The perfect companion to any meal, it may change your ideas about what is on offer – it's not all tapas and *paella*. Not only will this book help you to appreciate the true flavours of the country, it will enable you to cope with new or unfamiliar situations, taking the worry out of ordering what you want. This book is organised in the following chapters:

Food of Spain

Spain's regions are colourfully described, with the emphasis on local foods and specialities, and a look at the influences and traditions that are still detectable. A comprehensive A–Z covers both the foods you are likely to see in Spanish shops and markets and the dishes you will find on the menus.

Wine and Drink of Spain

Here you will find information and advice on wine, along with an A–Z of other drinks, both alcoholic and non-alcoholic.

Eating Out

The Eating Out section can help you decide where to eat and at what time. There are also tips on catering for babies and children, as well as for special diets.

Eating In

The guide to shopping describes the different types of shops, the services they offer and what you can buy (including picnic food). The recipes, using typical Spanish ingredients, will appeal to cooks of all abilities.

Practical Information

This chapter contains essential information such as managing a tight budget and planning a self-catering holiday. A short section also highlights the types of food and dishes eaten on high days and holidays and advises on what is seasonally available. Understanding the menu can sometimes be a problem, and the language section gives helpful phrases to use in a variety of shops and restaurants, as well as a pronunciation guide. Finally, there is a conversion table to help with shopping.

Food of Spain

The sunshine colours of a Spanish paella *make it a joy to behold – and to eat.*

Calamari *tastes wonderful, deep-fried and served simply with a slice of lemon.*

Food of Spain

For almost 1,000 years after its conquest by the Arabs in AD 711, Spain's cultural links were with North Africa. As the Arab Moors were driven out, however, they were replaced by a number of separate kingdoms. And though the country united in 1474, provinces such as the Basque country and Catalunya have continued to assert their individuality with great pride. This regionalism is certainly reflected in the cooking.

Another important factor that influenced the development of Spanish cookery was the discovery of America in 1492. From these exotic lands came a wealth of new and delicious foods such as chocolate, as well as tomatoes, peppers, potatoes, coffee, maize, sugar cane and numerous varieties of beans. The Spanish adopted them all and invented recipes to make use of them long before they became familiar elsewhere.

During the 16th century it was Italian chefs who would raise the reputation of the new Spanish restaurants. The French contribution came when *nouvelle cuisine* inspired the Basques to their own *nueva cocina vasca*. Spanish cooks adopted the aspects of the new style that suited them – the results were better versions of the local dishes that they had always made, lovingly produced with a new confidence. Today Spain is still home to some of the most highly regarded restaurants in the world, especially in Barcelona.

So, as you prepare for a trip to Spain, enjoy the thought that you are about to embark on a delicious culinary adventure. For a Spanish feast awaits you!

Regions

Spain is a country of fierce regional pride. Wherever you are, you will be told that just here in this particular corner of Spain, are found the best beans, or asparagus, or peppers in the world. The cooking is well matched to the ingredients and recipes are regional – or have developed regional variations.

ANDALUCÍA

In Andalucía you will find the essence of all that is Spain – flamenco dancing, bull-fighting and brown *sierras* (mountains) – often topped by the black bull silhouette that used to advertise Veterano Osborne brandy, and was left by the government as a cultural icon. It is a huge area of the south, cut off from central Spain by the Sierra Morena.

The Arabs marked the landscape by planting olives and oranges. They created a cuisine based on spices such as cumin and saffron, and ingredients such as olive oil and nuts, all ground with pestle and mortar. Their chilled soups, such as the white garlic and almond *ajo blanco*, made with local Muscat grapes, and *gazpacho* (now made with tomato, pepper, garlic and cucumber) are welcome in the summer heat. It is here that tapas were invented, to sustain evenings that end in a mere five hours' sleep. One of the best tapa is sliced *serrano*, raw ham cured above the winter snow line at places such as Trevélez.

The Costa del Sol is celebrated for its fried fish – indeed, the fried fish take-away was invented here in the great seaport of Cádiz – and the city is now known for its *pescaíto frito* (mixed fried fish), while each beach-bar on the coast offers squid rings in batter. Málaga is famous for deep-fried little *chanquetes* (gobies, or other tiny fish) and fresh anchovies, with their tails stuck together then fried in the shape of a fan. The area is also known for skate with paprika, grilled swordfish steaks and fish soups, such as *caldillo de perro*. A fish stew worth searching out is *urta a la roteña*.

From Jerez de la Frontera, where your sample of Fino is hurled through the air into a glass, come sherry dishes such as kidneys in sherry or stewed bull's tail (*rabo de toro a la jerezana*). In Seville, you can taste countless exquisite tapas dishes, such as *solomillo al whisky*.

Flamenco dancing is at the very heart of Andalucían identity.

Almond trees flourish in the warm Spanish sun.

Tomatoes and peppers were first introduced here 400 years ago and appear in many local dishes, such as *pipirrana* (pepper salad) and flamenco eggs, the colourful Gypsy mixture of different vegetables with eggs. Another traveller's dish is *olla gitana*, a stew that can include any vegetable or fruit.

Desserts in the south of Spain are eaten in small spoonfuls as they are incredibly sweet; examples are quince paste and *tocino de cielo*, a jelly of syrup and egg yolks.

The best, however, are the little Arab cakes, such as the almond *alfajores* of Medina Sidonia and the crumbly *polvorones* in Antequera. Try also the *yemas*, which are rich little egg yolk candies, and which were traditionally made by nuns.

LEVANTE

Its name means 'where the sun rises', and the Levante takes in most of the east coast, from Cartagena northwards. It encompasses the orange-growing areas of Alicante and Valencia – and a good many sunshine beaches, including Benidorm. This is the land that the legendary medieval hero El Cid won back from the Moors.

The Arabs introduced rice and Valencia is the home of the famous *paella* – originally cooked outdoors – and other rice and fish dishes, including *arroz a banda* and *el caldero*. Rice is also partnered with beans to good effect in the black and white dish *moros y cristianos* (meaning 'Moors and Christians').

The market gardens here produce wonderful vegetables, while the big Albufera lake yields both ducks and eels. *Anguila al ali-pebre* is a spicy way of serving the latter.

The most famous fish dish of this area is *dorada a la sal*, bass baked in salt, but the grey mullet is also good, as is an unusual brown mussel (*dantil de mar*). Other specialities include cured fish, such as *mojama* and *giraboix*, which is a salted cod stew. The coast is also a centre for pickled capers – delicious with fried fish.

As well as oranges, figs and Muscat grapes are plentiful, while Elche has the world's largest date grove. A milky summer drink to try is *horchata*, made from tiger nuts, while the whole of Spain buys almond *turrón* from Jijona at Christmas.

CATALUNYA AND THE BALEARICS

Catalunya (also known as Cataluña or Catalonia) embraces both the Pyrenees (Pirineos) and the Costa Brava. Barcelona's restaurants have been famous for over 100 years and the city is now regarded as one of Europe's best places to eat.

Zarzuela and *suquet*, two ebullient fish stews that burst with shellfish, are made here, as is the wonderfully crazy mixture *langosta con pollo* (lobster with chicken), while *langosta a la catalana* is likely to be lobster with chocolate!

Parrillada is a grilled dish that includes fish and shellfish (or fish with meat), often with chilli and nut *romesco* sauce. Salted cod is so popular here that it is sold ready-soaked, to make dishes such as *xató*, the Tarragona salad. Or try the pasta and shellfish mix called *fideuà*. Duck with figs, or gosling with pears, are characteristic poultry and fruit combinations, while duck with olive, and rabbit with snails are other celebrated pairings. Vich is known for its *charcuterie*, and excellent black and white *butifarra* sausages are made here.

Grills are a speciality, including *costellada*, lamb chops with local sausage, eaten with pungent *alioli* (garlic sauce). Indeed, barbecues produce some of the best food, including *escalivada* (baked whole vegetables), barbecued spring onions eaten at the feast called *calçotada*, and grilled snails, eaten at the *cargolada* feast. In winter, warming vegetable stews such as *escudella de pagés* are a welcome feast, and wild mushrooms, particularly *rovellón*, are a passion.

Well-prepared spinach, *espinacas a la catalana*, is eaten with the flat bread called *coca*. And you will find that in Catalunya all meals start with a tomato bread called *pan tomaca*.

The English occupied Menorca in the Balearic Isles (Islas Baleares) in the 18th century – and left gin and gravy (*grevi*) behind as proof! The French, on the other hand, found *mahonesa* (mayonnaise) there in the 1770s, and took the recipe home.

But the Balearics are best known for very solid, heavy dishes made with lots of bread, such as *sopa mallorquina*, and vegetable stews such as *tumbet*. Stuffed squid, fried poultry in sauce (*escaldums*), and *sobrasada* (a soft red sausage spread) are other local dishes. The pizza-like *cocas mallorquinas* are traditionally baked in outdoor ovens, and pies, large and small, are island favourites. There is a local cheese, too – Mahón.

Catalunya gave the world a favourite dessert, *crème brûlée* (*crema catalana*), but try also the almond cream (*menjar blanco*), and simple curds with honey (*mel i mató*). *Panellets* and *roscos* in Barcelona and *bunyols* on the coast are among the little cakes to look out for.

NEW CASTILE AND LA MANCHA

High on Spain's central plateau, this is Don Quixote and windmill country, centred on the nation's capital. The temperatures here are extreme – bitter winter cold and parching summer heat.

Madrid is home to all styles of cooking, with many good authentic regional restaurants. It also has a robust nightlife. Its most famous meat dishes are *cocido madrileño*, where several meats are simmered together for a few hours with chickpeas, and a beloved nursery dish of stewed tripe (*callos*) found in all the tapas bars. You will also find good roast meat, baked bream (*besugo al horno*) and a local salted cod dish, *soldaditos de pavía*. To the south, near the exquisite former royal summer palace at Aranjuez, strawberries and asparagus grow.

Castile (Castilla) is the country's bread basket, growing excellent wheat, which is very pure; from it a distinctive round bread is made – and also wheat soup. The bread is the ideal accompaniment to the local tomato stew (*pisto manchego*). Beans and lentils are the local crops. The plains

Spain's vineyards are not only productive, but also, as seen here, often picturesque.

also grow Spain's 'yellow gold' – saffron, the world's most expensive spice. And it is said that *tortilla*, the national egg dish, has its origins in Castile, invented by a peasant for a hungry king.

Castile is the partridge capital of Spain. The bird is used for *perdiz estofada* (braised partridge) and jellied *escabeche*, besides mixed game pâtés such as *gazpacho manchego* and *morteruelo*.

The plains are famous for sheep, and for the country's most distinguished cheese, Manchego. Try it breadcrumbed and fried as *queso frito*. Madrid fiestas are well known for their sweet pastries, including the cream-filled *buñuelos* and the sugared bread *torrija*, made for children. Toledo, the old capital, is famous for *mazapán*, fashioned into little *figuras* for Christmas. The wine-soaked cakes, *bizcochos borrachos*, can be eaten in any season.

OLD CASTILE AND RIOJA

Cut off from Madrid to the south by the Guadarrama mountains (Sierra de Guadarrama), Old Castile runs north to the Cordillera Cantábrica. Three of Spain's great medieval cities are sited here – Ávila, Salamanca and Segovia.

Strings of garlic bulbs for sale at the Aragónese town of Jaca.

This is the centre of the *zona de asados*, for here the best roasts are prepared in the old beehive Arab ovens, called *hornos de asar*, which are characteristic of Segovia, Valladolid and Burgos. The secret is that the meat is not cooked quickly, as you might expect for young animals; instead, it is roasted gently and slowly for extra succulence. At Ávila and Segovia, *cochinillo* (suckling pig) is an institution, though the *lechal* (milk-fed lamb) is sometimes rated even higher.

Zamora is known as chickpea country. The Rioja also grows wonderful peppers; indeed, dishes with *a la riojana* in their name are likely to include peppers, as in, for example, *patatas a la riojana* (potatoes Rioja-style). Lots of beans are grown and eaten dried, as well as fresh, and fresh beans (*pochas*) are also eaten with quail or sausage. Baked aubergines (eggplants) and white asparagus, sold in cans throughout Spain, are other specialities.

Castilian garlic soup is also well known, especially at Ávila. The monastery there also makes the sugary yellow cakes called *yemas* (*yemas de Santa Teresa* are named after Ávila's patron saint).

ARAGÓN AND NAVARRA

Aragón and Navarra embrace the northern end of the Pyrenees and their foothills, a country dotted with monasteries, for pilgrims poured through Roncesvalles and other valleys on the pilgrim route to Santiago de Compostela, one of Europe's holiest Catholic shrines. With them they brought French-style dishes such as *menestra de verduras* (a type of vegetable stew). Another simple traveller's dish is salted cod in *bacalao al ajoarriero*.

Mountains mean good lamb, which here is served grilled as chops, roasted young as *ternasco*, or stewed as *cochifrito*. Be aware, though, that here 'mountain asparagus' means lambs' tails, which are cropped in spring! Real asparagus grows at Tudela and is used in the *tortillas*. The foothills slope down to the banks of the warm Ebro River, where red peppers are grown, in particular, the slim and very spicy *pimientos del piquillo*. At Lodosa these peppers are even protected by an *appellation contrôlée*, and they are eaten stuffed with meat or served with salted cod. The region is even better known for its red pepper stews called *chilindrones*.

Fast streams in the mountains breed trout, and *truchas a la Navarra* are fried in ham fat and served stuffed or wrapped in ham. The opening of the hunting season is celebrated with *pochas con codornices*, the first quails, eaten with fresh kidney beans. Partridges are often deliciously served with chocolate sauce. Rabbit is stewed with garlic, wine and rosemary, while fried sausages with eggs are popular, too.

The black Aragón *morcilla* (blood sausage) includes both rice and pine nuts, while the *chorizo* of Pamplona-Irunea is quite simply the best tapa sausage.

Hidden in the Pyrenees, the Val d'Arran was once cut off from the rest of Spain for six months of the year by bad weather until Franco built a tunnel to it. Now skiing has made the area fashionable, and good chefs have rushed to open *bordas*, 'barn restaurants', where the food is earthy but invariably good. Local specialities include pigeon with raisins and pine nuts (*pichón con pasas y piñones*).

Aragón has its own cheese in Roncal. It is also known for junket (*cuajada*), sold in brown pots resembling flowerpots and eaten with honey. The foothills bear orchards of apple, cherry and peach, and peaches in red wine are a delicious local delicacy.

BASQUE COUNTRY AND CANTABRICAN COAST

In their tiny corner of Spain, snuggled next to the Bay of Biscay (Golfo de Vizcaya) and the mountains that lead to France, the Basques are self-styled 'gourmets', with a restaurant for every thousand inhabitants. Here men-only associations, called *cofradías*, cook and eat gourmet meals – the women wash up! Anywhere in Spain, a Basque name on a restaurant (an unpronounceable title with 'TX' in it) means it is likely to be first-rate.

The Basques have traditionally looked outwards, beyond their own territory, for influence and inspiration. First, there is a French Basque region, too – as dishes such as the soft, un-Spanish omelette *piperrada* bear witness. Then Basques are the rovers, the Atlantic fishermen bringing home great catches of cod. Their shipboard stews such as *marmitako*, and other dishes made with Bonito tuna are well known. Among dozens of salted cod recipes, *bacalao a la vizcaína* is the most famous.

The area is also celebrated for the most delicate fish dishes, including *merluza en salsa verde* (hake in a green parsley and pea sauce), exquisite fried sole, and *bacalao al pil-pil*, requiring an especially light chef's touch. The name *donostia* (Basque for San Sebastián), is given to many local dishes, so expect to be a little confused. Other fishy luxuries are *txangurro* (stuffed crab) and *chipirones en su tinta*, best here when the squid are line-caught, not in nets, where they lose the ink that makes the black sauce of the dish.

Eating *angulas* (elvers) in winter started in the Basque eating clubs, and the fashion spread. Another rarity is *kokotxas*, pieces of hake cut from the throat, best made into fritters.

The Cantabrican coast, where many Spanish families take their holidays, is known for its small fish restaurants. Dishes include clams or baby sardines in sauces, and fresh local trout and salmon. *Raba* is an unusual squid dish, with the squid first coated in breadcrumbs, then fried.

The green Basque countryside grows fresh peas, green beans and artichokes in season, made into casseroles such as *menestra*. It is also known for broad beans, eaten fresh. Dried beans (such as kidney beans) are made into soups, including *baba-txikis*, or stewed with sausage, as in the bean stew of Tolosa. Guernica is famous for *choricero* peppers, used to make local sausages and roast peppers with chops. The Basques also make a good leek and potato soup with salted cod (*purrusalda*).

Local meat is good, with plentiful roasts, enormous steaks and good lamb and game dishes, such as *codornices en hojas* (quails in vine leaves). The Cantabrican coast is known for chicken with rice (*campurriano*). This is also dairy country, however, and the local Basque cheese is smoky Idiazábal, while a mild blue Pasiego is made at Pas. Desserts to tempt include custard horns (*cañutillos*) and *intxaursalsa*, an unusual walnut cream.

GALICIA AND ASTURIAS

The extreme northwest is Spain's Celtic fringe – a misty, green, apple-growing country. The landscape is studded with little *horreos*, sheds built on stilts for storing maize and cheeses. In the far west, the vines are grown up on pergolas, which is unusual for Spain. In the western bays, huge, tender orange mussels grow beneath structures that resemble Chinese junks, and indeed the whole area is famous for its seafood. Dishes that any visitor should try include *langosta*, the excellent lobster, while Santiago de Compostela has its own lobsters (*santiaguiños*) and of course the pilgrims' scallop dish, *vieiras de santiago*. A strange and costly shellfish is the tubular black barnacle, *percebes*. *Mariscada* is a shellfish feast. At festival time, large octopuses are displayed on all the bars, to be served as spicy *pulpo al feria*. *Rape* (monkfish, called *pixin* here) is cooked in cider. Varieties of fish are placed in layers to make a delicious *caldereta*,

These lobsters, on the quayside of the port of Luarca, are as fresh as can be.

19

A whitewashed village in the Extremaduran municipality of Casares de las Hurdes.

while small cuttlefish and sardines are made into pies. Freshwater fish include salmon.

This is tripe and sausage country, home of the black *morcilla* of León, which goes into Asturias' famous bean dish, *fabada*. Lentils and chestnuts are also much used. Galicia's best-known stew is *lacón con grelos*, a ham knuckle cooked with young turnip tops.

Butter and lard are much used in cooking, and a number of meats are cooked in milk. Duck with turnips is claimed as a Galician recipe, and chicken tastes excellent when roasted in pork fat or cooked with beans or rice. There are also many pigeon and partridge dishes. In the wilderness of Asturias, game such as chamoix and capercaillie is hunted. Local cuisine is simple fare – chestnut soup and *cachelada*, a stew with fine potatoes and *chorizo*, are good examples. Huge heads of cabbage, some a metre (3 feet) high, will catch your eye as you drive through Galicia, and these go into broths such as *caldo gallego*. Many lettuces are grown in this part of Spain, while locals claim watercress was first eaten here. The tiny green peppers from Padrón are sold all over Spain, usually deep-fried whole. Take care: as the saying goes, 'Some are hot, others are not'.

Empanadas are giant pies made with peppers and tomatoes, plus fish or pork, and further inland they may be topped with bread dough, rather than pastry. Rye bread is a local speciality, while cornmeal is used for bread (*borona*) sometimes stuffed with meat (*prenada*).

Spain's most famous creamy blue cheese, Cabrales, comes from Asturias, and distinctive fresh *requesones* (cottage cheeses) are made. Favourite cheeses include Galician smoked San Simón, which looks like an amber pear, and the soft, breast-shaped Tetilla.

Asturias is known for the best milk in Spain and not surprisingly you can enjoy many milk puddings: rice travelled north as *arroz con leche*. Look out too for the varieties of sweet pancake, such as the Galician liqueur-flavoured *filloas*. About 250 varieties of apples are grown locally, together with plums and pears. Desserts include apple tarts, pears in red wine with cinnamon (invented here), and superb sugary *marrón glacés*.

EXTREMADURA

The name means 'extreme and hard' and the west of the region, bordering Portugal, has some of the most beautiful mountain scenery in this mountainous country. Chestnuts, cork oaks and the evergreen holm oak, whose acorns feed the black pigs, grow in abundance.

The most famous ham in Spain is produced at Jabugo, where the snows of the sierras give it its popular name, *serrano* – 'mountain' ham. The best hams are those from the wild *pata negra* pig. Superb hams are also made at Montánchez. As you might expect, there are also excellent *chorizos* and *morcillas*. In a restaurant, an *entremeses de carne*, a sliced selection, is one way to try the local cured meat. Sausages also go into the local *tortilla*, while *pringadas* are bread strips fried in bacon fat. Garlicky *croûtons*, called *migas*, are made to eat with savoury dishes, and also served as a sweet with a chocolate sauce.

Local delicacies include frogs, small eels, partridge and turkey, while the monastery at Alcántara is famous for its luxury pheasant dish (*faisán al modo de alcántara*). Mountain lamb is the meat in the stew *cochifrito*; use is also made of tongues and liver, and there is a local kidney dish, *riñonada*. Jellied *escabeche* and freshwater tench are also relished.

A–Z of Spanish Food

A

Abadejo
Pollack. A fish similar to cod, but cooked like hake.

Abichón
Silverside or sand smelt. A good fish when tiny and deep-fried like whitebait.

Acedias fritas
Fried baby soles. A popular tapa in the southwest.

Aceite de girasol
Sunflower oil.

Aceite de oliva
Olive oil. Usually 'pure' (which is a mixture of virgin and refined oil) and labelled with its acidity – 0.8° is perfect.

Aceite de oliva virgen
Olive oil containing no refined oil. Its taste is spectacular and it is used raw in salads or with goats' cheese, or *pan tomaca*.

Aceitunas
Olives. *Aceitunas aliñadas* are marinated olives, that is, cocktail olives.

Aceitunas rellanas
Stuffed olives; these may come with red peppers or as *violadas*, which are big olives stuffed with gherkins.

Aceitunas rellenas con anchoas
Green olives with anchovy stuffing. The newest and nicest of the cocktail olives.

Acelga
Swiss chard or spinach beet. A vegetable with gleaming white stems and bitter dark leaves, which is much loved in the south. You will find it *fritas* and *guisadas* (fried and stewed); in *menestra*, a general vegetable stew; with potatoes; or in rice and bean soup; and as a *torta*, which may have a little sugar added to it as well.

Acelgas con pasas y pinoñes
Chard fried with plump raisins and crisp pine nuts, sometimes called *a la catalana*. *Acelgas a la malagueña* is boiled chard that is then stir-fried with garlic and paprika.

Achicoria
Chicory.

Ácido
Acid, as an adjective it means bitter.

Aderezada
With dressing. Many canned, cooked vegetables are sold like this.

Aderezo de mesa
Condiments.

Colourful black and green olives with red chillies and onions.

Adobo
Marinated before cooking. *Lomo adobado* is marinated pork loin for roasting or frying.

Agrio
Sour.

Agua de azahar
Orange flowered water. For flavouring desserts.

Aguacate
Avocado. *Con gambas* means it is stuffed with prawns.

Aguja
Long salty or sweet pastry, filled with minced meat or cream. (See also next entry.)

Aguja
Gar or needlefish. This fish is a couple of feet (60cm/2ft) long and has a nose like a knitting needle. The backbone is green,

but do not let this bother you – it is good poached. (See also previous entry.)

Aguja de ternera
Beef steak. From the shoulder area.

Agujas, en
On skewers.

Ahumado
Smoked. As in *salmón ahumado*.

Ajada, allada
Garlic, paprika, oil and bread beaten to make a sauce. Used to dress hot fish and vegetables.

Ajedrea
Savory (the herb).

Ajetes or Ajipuerros
A springtime speciality of young garlic shoots, pulled from the centre of the bulb. Wonderful with scrambled eggs, they are also pickled as *brotes de ajo*.

Aji
Red chilli pepper.

Ajiaceite, al, or Ajoaceite
In garlic oil. The simplest of Spanish sauces, which is used, for example, with snails.

Ajillo, en
In a garlic sauce, usually a pan sauce. Often thickened after frying with garlic puréed with bread.

Ajo
Garlic.

Ajoaceite
The same as *ajiaceite*. In Castilian it can mean *alioli*, usually a smooth dense garlic sauce, with eggs yolks and even mashed potato or breadcrumbs.

Ajo, al
The dish has whole garlic cloves in it. Do not be too frightened of these; garlic becomes quite mild after long cooking.

Ajo arriero
'In the mule-drivers' style', that is, dressed with garlic, paprika and parsley. These chaps were the forerunners of truckers, moving goods across the country. The places they stayed in *en route* were too poor for anything fancy, and these dishes are simple, made with eggs, or vegetables such as cauli-flower, or salted cod.

Ajo blanco
A most delicious chilled almond cream soup (white *gazpacho*) flavoured with garlic and finished with Muscat grapes or melon.

Ajo colorado
Creamy salted cod pounded with bread and garlic and coloured red with paprika. It is a red version of the French *brandade*, which indicates a food for Lent.

Ajo de la mano, el
Literally 'garlic in the hand' or 'garlic from the mortar', this is, potatoes cooked with chillies, then dressed with pounded garlic, cumin, oil and vinegar.

Ajonjolí
Sesame seeds. Popular in little festival cakes.

Ajopollo, en
'In the sort of garlic sauce chicken is served in', with almonds and normally with potatoes; see *pepitoria de gallina*.

Alajú
A rich, flat medieval cake. Dense, very dark and made with honey and whole toasted almonds, often with pine nuts or chestnuts, similar to *alfajores*, and like Italian *panforte*.

Albacora
The long-finned tuna with white flesh. It is less dense than *atún*, and considered the best variety.

Albahaca
Basil.

Albardado
Barded (wrapped in fat or fat meat, eg ham), or battered/crumb-coated.

Albaricoque

Apricot. Dried fruits are called *orejones*.

Albóndigas en salsa

Meatballs in sauce, usually tomato. A popular tapa, they are often made of veal and pork. The same word is often used for fish cakes. *Albóndigas de choco* (cuttlefish) is a delicious Huelva speciality.

Albufera, salsa

Mushroom, cream and red pepper sauce, sometimes with ground almonds in it. Good with fish.

Alcachofas

The big flower buds of globe artichokes. In the middle of each one is a bristly choke (which has to be removed) above the edible soft base. Prepared bases are often served as salads. *Aliñadas* means 'marinated' and *con mayonesa* is with mayonnaise. They are also included in many salads and hot rice mixtures.

Alcachofas a la vinagreta

Artichokes served boiled and warm, or cold, with vinaigrette. To eat, the leaves are pulled off, each base dipped into the sauce, then just the soft flesh pulled off with the teeth.

Alcachofas rellenas

Artichokes stuffed in the middle, often *con atún* (tuna).

Alcachofas salteadas con jamón

Sautéed artichoke bases with ham. The bases are also braised in Montilla, or served with potatoes, in a saffron broth (see recipe, pages 134–5).

Alcaparras

Capers. These grow wild, and the pickled flower buds are particularly good with fried fish, or as part of a typical dish of pork tongue (*lengua de cerdo*).

Alcaravea

Caraway seeds.

Alfajores

An individually wrapped Christmas almond and honey candy, invented by the Arabs. Those made in Medina Sidonia and Estepa are sensational.

Aliño

A simple vinaigrette, or an oil and salt dressing. *Aliñado* means marinated, or dressed, vegetables or fish.

Alioli (all-i-oli)

This is one of the greatest Spanish sauces, to be tried at least once in a lifetime. Take your vote that either everybody in your party eats it or nobody does, because it is fairly potent, containing puréed raw garlic as the main ingredient. This is whisked to an emulsion with oil and sometimes egg yolks too. The most common match is with boiled potatoes (*patatas al alioli*). One of the best sauces for prawns barbecued in the shell and grilled fish or chops, it is also stirred into

A Catalan salad of mixed vegetables and sausage is topped off with a spear of asparagus.

fish soups. In Catalunya, *aliolis* of puréed fruit and garlic are served with roast lamb.

Almadrote

A sauce of mashed garlic and hard cheese, usually cooked with aubergine (eggplant).

Almejas

Clams. Raw or cooked in wine or spicy tomato sauce, clams are popular seaside fare, though they are somewhat fiddly to eat. In *almejas con arroz*, clams and onions are used to flavour rice.

Almejas a la marinera

Clams fisherman-style, with white wine, a little oil and parsley.

Almendras, tostadas

Toasted almonds. They are popular with drinks. Everything from soup (*sopa*) to trout (*trucha*) can be served *almendrada*, made from or cooked with almonds. See *pepitoria de gallina* for almond sauce with chicken. *Almendras garrapiñadas* are almonds in toasted sugar.

Almíbar, en

In syrup. The Arabs invented syrup, and probably peaches in syrup too.

Alpargatas

The name means *espadrilles* and these 'shoe-shapes' can be sweet biscuits in the north. They can also be meat patties, coated in whisked egg before frying, which gives them the appearance of rope-soled shoes.

Alubias

Dried kidney beans of lots of different colours. Tolosa is famous for black beans (*alubias negras*). Beans *a la vizcaína* are typical:

stewed with a little *tocino* (pork fat), onion, garlic and parsley.

Amanida
The Catalan word for salad. Probably an arranged salad including fish (normally cod) and meat, if it is *a la catalana*.

Amargo
Bitter.

Amargos, amarguillos
Little, dry Arab marzipan cakes. Typical in Sahagún, a town in León.

Amarillo, en
A yellow sauce, made from onions and saffron, thickened with egg yolks or flour.

Ametlles
Catalan for almonds; also delicious toasted almonds, coated in praline or chocolate.

Anacardos
Cashew nuts.

Anchoas
Canned anchovies. *En aceite* (in oil).

Andaluza, salsa
Andalucían sauce. Usually includes garlic, tomatoes, peppers and pumpkin. *A la andaluza* is with red peppers and tomato.

Añejo
Aged (of cheese etc.).

Angelote
Angelfish, and a small shark, with a tail like *rape*, but less good to eat.

Anguila
Freshwater eel. *Angula* is elver – baby eel. These look like silver spaghetti and are an expensive luxury in winter.

Anguila al ali-pebre
Valencian speciality of eels in an oil, paprika, saffron, garlic and almond sauce. (Also spelt *al all i pebre*.)

Angulas a la bilbaína or en cazuela
A Basque speciality of baby eels tossed in chilli oil and garlic and served from an earthenware casserole with wooden forks.

Anís
Aniseed. One of the great flavours of Spain, much used for biscuits by adding one of the many *anís*-flavoured liquors.

Anona
Custard apple.

Añojo
(Meat from) a one-year-old calf.

Apio
Celery; *ensalada de apio* is celery salad.

Araña or peje
Weever fish. For soup.

Arándano
Bilberry.

Arándano Agrio
Cranberry.

Arencas
Salted and pressed sardines, in the style of *arenques*.

Arenque
Herrings, usually fried simply.

Arenque ahumado
Kipper.

Arete

Red gurnard. A fish with firm white flesh, of good flavour and not-too-difficult bones. As it is slightly dry, it is best cooked in sauce.

Arrope

A grape juice or honey syrup. Used for sweetening wine and for simmering dried fruit.

Arrós/arroz

Rice (see box, below).

Asado

From the oven, so roasted. *Asadillo* is roasted, skinned peppers reheated in little dishes with garlic.

Atascaburras

On the east coast, this is a purée of salted cod with potato and pine nuts; it is similar to *brandada de bacalao*. It is also like the French *brandade*.

Atún

Blue-fin tuna. It is served as a treat rather than as an everyday fish, grilled in big (bloody) steaks or baked. It may be cooked, marinated and served cold (*escabeche*), or made into small hot pies (*empanadillas*). See also *albacora*, called *atún blanco*.

THE DIVERSITY OF RICE

Rice is used to make many simple dishes in Spain, such as *ensalada* (rice salad), and is combined with all sorts of different ingredients, including *butifarra* sausage, chicken giblets, fried bananas, fish, pig's cheek and trotters, and much more. In the north, rice dishes are called *arroz*, whereas they would be called *paella* in Valencia.

Arrós amb crosta (Catalan)/arroz con costra (Castilian) A famous *paella*, with meatballs, pieces of poultry and pork (leftovers from the *cocido*), cooked in the oven. The egg crust is broken when the dish is served.

Arroza a banda A famous two-course Valencian fish and rice dish. The rice, which is flavoured with saffron and fish stock, is served first. The fish, which were cooked in the stock, are then dished up to follow, often with *alioli*.

Arroz con leche A cold rice pudding, flavoured with lemon and cinnamon. Popular in the northwest. *Requemado* has a grilled sugar top.

Arroz negre Black rice. It is a speciality of the Costa Brava. Cuttlefish ink colours the rice.

Avellana

Hazelnuts. Popular in sauces and *pâtisserie*.

Avena

Oats.

Azafrán

Saffron. This Arab spice is much used in rice and stews in the north as well as in the south. It is always expensive, but beware of imitations.

Azahar

Orange blossom.

Azúcar

Sugar. *Azúcar moreno* is brown sugar – *azucarillos* is candy floss.

B

Bacalao

Cod. This is not a Mediterranean fish, though it may be fresh on the Atlantic coast. It is hugely popular salted and dried, and is much eaten at Lent. It does not taste salty after soaking and should be left for 24 hours in a bowl of cold water, under a dribbling tap. It soon makes the water smell, so the water must be changed regularly. Then, after removing all of the skin and bones, it can be cooked as fresh. In Catalunya, cod is called *bacallá* and is cooked *en samfaina* (in tomato sauce). It is good fried in fingers (*soldaditos*), and makes tasty *buñuelos* (deep-fried potato puffs) and wonderful salads such as *esqueixada*.

Bacalao al ajo arriero

Salted cod mashed with garlic and parsley. It is always a pale dish, but can contain scrambled egg.

Bacalao a la vizcaína

The most famous hot dish made with salted cod. The sauce includes the piquant peppers of the region and sweet *ñora* chillies. Well-made, it is wonderful, but it can also be pretty grim: fish, pools of oil and sparse, too-spicy pepper. Outside the Basque country, the sauce often includes tomatoes, too. *Bacalao al la riojana* is very similar, made with peppers and paprika.

Bacalao pil-pil

A Basque dish of hot salted cod. It is gently rocked in the casserole until the gelatine from the fish makes an emulsion, and so produces a very light white sauce, just from cooking oil and garlic, and sometimes *guindilla* (chilli pepper). Served very hot.

Baifo

The name given to kid in some Canarian dishes.

Bajoques farcides

Red peppers stuffed with rice and meat or *bacalao*.

Banderilla

A cocktail stick with bits of cheese or ham; named after the barbed stick used in the bullfight.

Baño María al
A double saucepan for boiling, or a *bain marie*.

Barbacoa, a la
Barbecued.

Barquillo
A thin rolled wafer, made on a mould.

Barra de pan
The typical long loaf of bread, similar to a French *baguette*, but wider. The most common is a *pistola* (literally, a 'pistol'). At the bakery, ask for: '*Una pistola, por favor.*'

Bartolillos
Triangles filled with custard, then deep-fried – a speciality of Madrid.

Batata
Sweet (white) potato.

Becadas
Woodcock. These are roasted or pot-roasted and may be stuffed with their own gizzards, or they may be pounded for sauce.

Becerro
Baby *ternera*, or calf.

Beicon, bacon
Leanish pink breakfast bacon.

Bellota
Acorn, the fruit of the oak. The best *serrano* ham is called *jamon de Bellota* because it is made from free-range pigs fed exclusively on cork oak and holm oak acorns.

Berberechos
Cockles. Less sweet than clams, they are made into sauces or served in soup or rice.

Berenjenas
Aubergines (eggplants). Introduced by the Arabs. *Al horno* is baked, *fritas* is fried and they are also moulded (*molde*).

Berenjenas a la catalana
Fried aubergines (eggplants) cooked in tomato sauce.

Berenjenas rellenas
Stuffed aubergines (eggplants) with minced beef as well as garlic, breadcrumbs and chopped egg, or sometimes with fish.

Berros
Watercress.

Berza
Green cabbage. Often included in soups or *menestra*. *Bertón* is a stuffed cabbage.

Berza andaluza
As happens sometimes in Spanish cooking, the 'Andalucían cabbage' usually doesn't include cabbage at all, but is rather a mixture of chickpeas or dried beans with celery, *acelga* or green beans, flavoured with salt pork or other bits of the pig.

Besugo
Red bream, which has a black spot on the shoulder. This is a favourite fish in Spain, and is good grilled or baked with lemon and oil or in white wine (*al vino blanco*).

Besugo a la donastiarra
Red bream baked with garlic, vinegar and *guindilla* (red chilli).

Besugo a la Madrileña
Red bream, usually baked with white wine over a bed of potatoes and onions.

Besugo asado con piriñaca
Bream baked with Andalucían red pepper salad.

Bien me sabe
Means 'tastes good to me' and given as an excuse to eat something delicious. The name of a fish dish (see *cazón en adobo*) and also a very rich Andalucían dessert of ground almonds and cinnamon.

Biftek, bistek
Beef steak. Ask for it *poco hecho* for rare, *al punto* for medium or *muy hecho* for well-done.

Biftek salteado al jerez
Fried steak with a little sherry used to make a sauce with the cooking juices.

Bizcocho
Sponge cake. The word is used to cover all types, even sponge finger biscuits. It may be *de almendras* (almonds), *de chocolate*, *al limón* (lemon) or *a la crema* (cream).

Bizcochos borrachos
'Drunken' cakes soaked in wine or syrup, then sugared.

Bocadillo
A sandwich of a crusty roll, sprinkled inside with olive oil and often filled with ham and cheese. *Tortilla*, *chorizo* or *lomo* (pork) are also very common.

Bocadillos de monja
This 'nun's mouthful', is a small cake made of almonds, sugar and eggs.

Bocadito
A 'mouthful' – often found on biscuit packets.

Bogovante
The true lobster.

Bola
Béchamel-based croquette, served deep-fried.

Boletus
Cep mushrooms.

Bolets amb pernil
A simple dish of ceps and ham.

Bollo
A common word for a bread roll, also a sweet bun; (see also *suizos*). *Bollos de panizo* is a cornmeal scone, eaten with vegetables. *Bollo preñado* – 'pregnant roll' – has meats cooked inside.

Bomba
Meatball, or potato shape, served with chilli sauce.

Bombón
A chocolate.

Boniato
The orange-fleshed sweet potato: America's 'yam'. It is made into sweet puddings with cinnamon; or cooked then dipped into syrup; it is also puréed.

Bonito
Means 'pretty', and this light, white-fleshed tuna, with a dark striped back, is highly prized. It is good grilled or baked, and makes *marmitako*.

Boquerones
Fresh anchovies. They taste quite different from canned versions (*anchoas*). The best come from L'Escala. They are marinated and served pickled as an *ensalada or en vinagreta*.

Boquerones a la malagueña
Fresh anchovies stuck together at the tail to form a fan, then floured and fried.

Borona
Cornmeal bread. Traditional in Asturias and Cantabria.

Borra, la, borreta
A salted cod and potato soup with spinach, flavoured with sweet chilli.

Borracho
Grey gurnard (fish), with firm but dry white flesh. Best baked.

Borrachos, borrachuelos
These 'drunkards' are doughnuts or cakes soaked in wine or syrup. Typical in Málaga.

Bou estofat, buey estofado
Catalan beef stew, with sweet *rancio* wine, *butifarra*, potatoes and possibly wild mushrooms.

Bover
A large edible snail; see *caracoles*.

Brandada de bacalao
A cod and potato purée, good to spread over bread.

Brasa, a la
Grilled on a grid over the embers (*brasas*). Meat *a la brasa de sarmiento* is cooked over vine prunings. The best!

Brasear
To grill over live coals.

Brazo de gitano
'Gypsy's arm'. A well-known cake, like a Swiss roll, but brown, longer and thinner. It is rolled up with cream or chocolate custard. There is also a version made with potato.

Breca
Small bream. Good grilled or baked; see *dentón*.

Brécol, bróculi
Broccoli. It is called *Broquil* in Catalunya, where it is very popular.

Brevas
A black early-ripening fig. Also, small yeast doughnuts, deep-fried with a custard filling.

Brocheta
A skewer or spit.

Brotes
Sprouts, bean sprouts or, in the Basque country, the spring side shoots of cabbage.

Buey
Ox, so stewing beef.

Buey de mar
The big-clawed crab.

Buey estofado
Ox stew.

Bullit
The Mallorcan version of *cocido*, that is, a chickpea stew, which may contain fish instead of pork.

Buñuelos
Fried puffs, often served as tapas. The lightest versions are made of choux pastry, with additions – such as *buñuelos de queso* (cheese puffs). *Buñuelos de bacalao* are often based on mashed potato – a good way to try out salted cod. Others are coated, crisp fried morsels; for example, *sesos*, made with brains, which are very creamy inside, or *apio*, made from celery. Sweet fritters are made from apricot (*albaricoque*) and soaked in syrup (*al aguamiel*).

Buñuelos de viento
Choux puffs, which are 'as light as the wind' according to the name. These are typically served in several Spanish regions on All Saint's Day. San Isidro is celebrated in Madrid with cream-filled versions.

Bunyettes
Yeast doughnuts.

Bunyols
Warm, sugared, deep-fried doughnuts. Popular on the Costa Brava, sometimes cream-filled.

Burgos, queso de
A fresh ewes' milk cheese, a bit like a drum-shaped Mozzarella, but milder in taste and softer to the touch.

Búsano
Whelk.

Boquerones en vinagreta, *the ever-popular Spanish fish dish.*

Butifarra

A big banger, the white sausage made from pork or veal, of Catalunya. It is frequently cooked with beans (*con habas*). There are also black *butifarrones*.

Butifarra amb mongetes

Catalan *butifarra* sausage stewed with dried white beans.

C

Caballa

Common mackerel. An oily fish, best baked (*al horno*) – it is good *a la gaditana* – or stewed with potatoes. See also *estornino*.

Cabello de ángel

'Angel's hair' comes from a squash (*cidra*), with very stringy flesh. It is stewed or made into a popular jam, much used in shop pastries.

Cabeza de ternera

A 'head-cheese' (ie a seasoned loaf) of jellied veal. *Cabeza de cerdo* is brawn.

Cabra

Goat. Both *cabrito asado* (young goat) and *caldereta de cabra* (stewed kid) are good.

Cabracho

The ugly, spiny, copper-red scorpion fish. A great soup-stew ingredient. (See also *escorpena*.)

Cabrales

A creamy blue cheese. A cheese to challenge Roquefort, and, also like it, one that is stored in limestone caves, where it acquires its blue veining. It is generally made of cows' milk and shaped like a small drum without pressing. It is finally wrapped in maple leaves.

Cabrilla

Comber (fish). It is used for soup, although the tail is also worth eating.

Cabrillas

In Andalucía, large snails, usually cooked with tomatoes.

Cabrito

Baby kid.

Cacahuetes

Peanuts.

Cachelada

A Galician stew using the new potatoes called *cachelos* with *chorizo* or ham.

Cailón

Porbeagle shark. Good to eat, especially the barbecued steaks.

Calabacines

Courgettes. They are baked (*al horno*), stuffed (*rellenos*) and made into fritters (*fritos*).

Calabaza guisada

Stewed pumpkin, often included in vegetable sauces in the south.

Calabazote

A sweet pumpkin dessert.

Calamares

Squid. Batter-fried squid rings (*a la romana*) are a common tapa. Small squid are cooked in their own ink, *en su tinta*, in the north – see *chipirones*. In the south, small *calamaritos* are served in a tomato, pepper, paprika and fish sauce.

Calamares rellenos

Stuffed squid. The stuffing may be pork and almonds (*a la catalana*), or cheese with pine nuts, bread-crumbs and parsley (*a la levantina*); in Mallorca raisins are added.

Calçots

A Catalan word for spring onions as thick as a finger, which are a speciality of Valls in Tarragona. At *la calçotada*, a spring feast, they are eaten direct from the barbecue with *romesco* sauce.

Caldereta de cordero

Stewed lamb. This is particularly good when thickened by the lamb's liver. In Extremadura it also includes red peppers, garlic, paprika, *migas* (fried breadcrumbs) and the local sausage as well; in Seville, a good slug of sherry is added. There are also quail (*codornices*) and rabbit (*conejo*) versions.

Caldereta de pescado

On the north coast, this is layered fish casserole, often with potatoes, and there are versions with shellfish and even lobster (*langosta*). These may be served liquid first, as soup, then as a fish dish.

Caldero

A cooking pot or small cauldron. *Caldereta, caldeirada* are the stews made in a *caldero. El caldero* on the south coast is a soupy rice and fish dish.

Caldillo de perro

Little 'dog soup'. It is made of fresh small hake and potatoes, flavoured with bitter orange juice and is a speciality of Puerto de Santa María on Cádiz harbour.

Caldo gallego

A hearty Galician soup, containing white beans or potatoes and chard, turnip tops and a ham bone.

Caliente

Hot (temperature).

Callos

Stewed tripe. Popular in tapas bars across Spain.

Callos a la catalana

Stewed tripe dish that may include pine nuts and rich *rancio* wine.

Callos a la madrileña

Typical stewed tripe dish. Highly spiced with ham and *chorizo*. Chickpeas are often included, as they are in Galicia and Andalucía.

Camarones

Tiny shrimp, white in Cádiz. Typical in *tortilla de camarones* (see recipe, page 131), a flour-based fritter.

Camerano, queso de

A soft, fresh goats' milk cheese from Rioja.

Campurriano

'From the country' of Cantabria (Santander). *Pollo campurriano* in Santander is a rice dish with

If you eat in a Spanish country restaurant, you may well find snails – caracoles – on offer.

chicken, bacon, peppers, shallots and wine. *Galletas campurrianas* are Cantabrian-style biscuits.

Caña de Azucar or caña dulce
Sugar cane.

Caña de vaca
Marrow bone.

Cañadilla, cañailla
Sea snail, like a whelk with knobs on. Eaten cold as a starter. This is the *murex* from which the Roman Imperial purple dye came. It will not stain your mouth though, as the dye develops only when exposed to the sun.

Canela, con
Meaning, 'with cinnamon'. This spice goes into many savoury dishes and replaces vanilla as the main flavouring of custard, ices and chocolate desserts. In Spain

it is usually included in biscuits and cakes.

Canelones
Cannelloni, stuffed and covered in sauce. In Spain, they are sold either as roll-them-yourself squares of pasta, or frozen and ready-made.

Canelones a la barcelonesa
Cannelloni stuffed with ham and chicken livers (*foie gras* if you are lucky), in a tomato sauce and sherry sauce. They are then topped with *béchamel* sauce and grilled.

Cangrejo (de mar)
The large-clawed crab.

Cangrejos de río
Freshwater crayfish. Messy to eat, but very good, cooked with tomato, brandy and chilli, called *a la Soriana* ('in Soria's style').

Canónigos
Lamb's lettuce or corn salad.

Cantabria, queso de
A flattish round cheese, semi-hard and made from cows' cream in a celebrated cheese area in the north.

Cañutillos de crema
Pastry custard horns.

Cap roig
Scorpion fish (in Catalan, 'red head'). Can be baked if it is large, but it is mostly used for soup; see *escorpena*.

Capirotada, la
Meat hidden by a 'hood' of almond sauce. The dish was commonly made from partridge, but it may also be made from rabbit, chicken or other small birds; it is sometimes also made from meatballs.

Capitón
Type of grey mullet; see *lisa*.

Caqui
Kaki or persimmon, a winter tree fruit. Very acidic unless it is soft, yellow and like an over-ripe tomato.

Carabineros
Enormous, showy scarlet prawns with purplish heads, named after their military colouring. They are not as tasty as *langostinos*, being a bit bland, so their flavour is boosted with brandy. They are often made into soup.

Caracoles
Snails. A popular country food, often just served with vinegar.

Sin trabajo means out of their shells – literally, 'no work'.

Carajitos
Hazelnut macaroons.

Caramelos
Sweets.

Carbonero
The black-backed coalfish, coley or saithe. Cooked like *merluza*.

Cardamomo
Cardamom.

Cardo
In general, this means thistle. In cooking terms, it refers to the artichoke thistle, or cardoon, related to the globe artichoke, though the stalks are blanched in plastic, rather like celery. These are eaten in white sauce, often with ham, or braised.

Cargolada, la
A snail feast in Catalunya; *cargol* is a snail.

Cari
Curry.

Carn d'olla
See *escudella*.

Carne
Meat; this means beef if it is without further description. *Carne de ternera* (veal) is the main Spanish beef. Argentinian veal and its style of cut is very popular nowadays in Spain, served in Argentinian restaurants and also sold in markets. (*Carnicería* is a butcher's shop.) *Carne de buey* (ox) also makes good beef stews.

Carne de buey en estofado

A stew, usually with root vegetables. *A la catalana*, it may have *butifarra* (white sausage) and chocolate in it, and *con peras de castañas* is with pears, thickened with chestnuts.

Carne de lidia

Meat from a bull that has died in a bullfight. Dark red, tough and strong – not sold in ordinary butchers.

Carne picada

Minced meat.

Carnero

Mutton. Excellent *estofado* (braised) or *con ajo* (with garlic) for it has more flavour than young lamb.

Carnero verde

Mutton dish from Tenerife. Braised with chopped parsley, garlic, egg yolks, bacon, mint and lettuce heart, with lemon juice and spices.

Carquinyolis

Almond biscuit, made hard by slicing a loaf and rebaking the slices. Its crumbs are used for thickening meat sauces.

Carrillada

Pig's cheek. Stewed in sherry in the south.

Cártamo

Safflower, also called *alazor*. The false saffron – also bright yellow, but without the incomparable taste.

Casadielles

Little sweet puff pastry turnovers, filled with ground walnuts, then baked or fried. This is a speciality of Asturias.

Castañas

Chestnuts. They are made into a simple cream soup, flavoured with cinnamon, and are also cooked *con leche*, in milk, as a pudding with sugar. In winter they are delicious, sold baked, from street stalls.

Castañola

See *palometa* and *japuta*.

Caza

The 'hunt', so referring to game.

Cazón

The smooth-hound, one of the best edible sharks, because it feeds on shellfish. Its steaks are white, firm and somewhat dry.

Cazón en adobo

Seasoned in paprika and vinegar, then battered and deep-fried. Good in Cádiz and Seville.

Cazuela

This is Spain's commonest brown cooking pot. It gives its name to any stew that comes out of it. Little *cazuelitas* are much used for cooking individual portions of fish – with plenty of sauce – and for eggs and mushrooms.

Cebolla

Onion. *Cebollone* is the Castilian for *calçot*. *Cebolletas* are spring onions, while *cebollinos* are chives. *Encebollada* means 'in onion sauce'.

Cecina

Dried beef eaten raw like ham, ('jerky'), *ceniza* in Catalunya. There is also a tuna version (*mojama*).

Centeno

Rye. A black bread made in Galicia.

Centollo

Spider crab. There is enough meat for one person only on each crab, for its claws are small and empty. The flesh is stronger and sweeter than that of clawed crabs, so is often mixed with hake, brandy, parsley, garlic and lemon and stuffed back in to the shell. This may then be grilled.

Cerdo

Pork, the most common meat.

Cerezas

Cherries.

Cervera, queso de

A fresh ewes' and cows' milk cheese, made in Valencia.

Chacina

Minced pork or sausage filling. *Chacinería* are pork products – the Spanish *charcuterie*.

Chalotas

Shallots. Also called *ajo chalote* (from the French, *echalotte*).

Champiñones

Cultivated mushrooms. Often served *al ajillo* (with garlic) like wild varieties. They are good as *rellenos*, stuffed with sausage or pork and crumbs, or fried with ham.

Chanfaina

A stew eaten on the day of pig killing, the *matanza*. It contains the lungs, head and other parts of the pig with the liver. However, do not confuse this with dishes such as *pollo en chanfaina*, which is chicken in *samfaina* sauce.

Changurro, txangurro

The Basque term for *centollo*, a popular potted tapa.

Chanquetes

The overfished whitebait, similar to gobies, slim silver fish nicknamed 'sea spaghetti', and a Málaga speciality. This is now a term for any tiny fried fish, battered and deep-fried.

Cherna

Wreckfish or stone bass, a grouper. Cooked like *mero*.

Chicharro

Coarse horse mackerel or scad. Best grilled.

Chicharrones

The crackling made from pork skin, left when fat is rendered. This is sold as a snack and is sometimes included in bread. Also called *cortezas de cerdo*.

Chipirones

Tiny squid. Good when stuffed with their own tentacles and served in a sauce of their own ink (*en su tinta*), or grilled *a la plancha* in the south.

Chirimoyas

Custard apples. Eat them with a spoon, spitting out the big seeds.

They are very smooth and creamy when ripe.

Choco

A small cuttlefish. Stewed *con habas* (with beans). Very good *a la plancha*, grilled with garlic, onions and peppers and spiced with saffron. *Papas con choco* are stewed with potatoes. *Albóndigas de choco* (cuttlefish meatballs) are a speciality in Huelva.

Chocolate

Chocolate is not particularly good in Spain, except in the Basque country. Bars of chocolate are poor quality; only the breakfast drink is good.

Chocolate, marquesa de

Chocolate mousse flavoured with cinnamon or orange.

Chopa

Red or black bream, also called *sargo*. Good to eat; see *dentón*. Excellent *a la sidra* (in cider).

Chopitos

Small cuttlefish, especially in Andalucía, where they are also called *puntillitas*; see also *sepia*.

Chorizo

The scarlet sausage, flavoured with *choricero* (chilli), which is sweet but not very hot. There are two types of sausage. The fatter version is the equivalent of salami, eaten sliced on bread. The other is stewed with beans and soups, or fried, and comes hot or mild.

Choto

Baby kid or *cabrito*; in some regions it is baby calf, also *becerro*. See also *cabra*.

Chufa

Tiger nut. This is the tuber of a type of sedge. Made into the chilled drink *horchata*, sometimes iced.

Chuletas de cerdo

Pork chops. Usually dusted with paprika or breaded and fried or grilled, then served with a little lemon juice.

Chuletas de cordero

Lamb chops served with garlic, parsley, rosemary, pine nuts or other ingredients. A luxury.

Chuletas de cordero a la navarra

Lamb chops in a sauce of ham or *chorizo*, onion and tomato.

Chuletas de cordero al sarmiento

Tiny (and expensive) lamb chops, grilled over vine prunings.

Chuletas de ternera

Veal chops, big and juicy. Best *a la riojana* (with roast red peppers), which is also a popular method of cooking pork chops.

Chuletón

An enormous wing rib beef chop. Beef is best in the north of Spain.

Chumbo or higo chumbo

Cactus fruit or prickly fig; a very refreshing fruit. The trick is to peel it with a knive and fork, avoiding the spines.

Churrasco

Means 'scorched', and so barbecued; often spare ribs.

Churros

Breakfast fritters. These ubiquitous fritters are sold in every market. The dough is piped in circles into the hot fat before your eyes. In Madrid, these rings are called *churros*, and a bigger, bar-shaped variety is called *porra*. In Seville you'll find ring-shaped versions, called *churropapa*, while the bigger, longer ones are the proper *churro*. The fritter rings may be threaded onto a reed for carrying, and sugared. Good with breakfast chocolate or coffee.

Cidra

A big squash with stringy flesh, made from the *cidra* fruit, which is similar to a lemon but a bit larger. It is boiled in sugar to make a popular jam; see *cabello de ángel*.

Ciervo

Deer. The meat is tough, so is best stewed with herbs.

Cigalas

Not to be missed, these are what the Italians call scampi and the British, Dublin Bay prawns or Norway lobster. There is some meat in the claws, but most is in the tail. Unlike other prawns, they are pink when raw. Eat them boiled or grilled, with coarse salt.

Cilantro, culantro

Coriander. Fresh leaves are used in the Canary Islands.

Ciruelas

Plums and greengages. *Ciruelas en aguardiente* are bottled in *eau-de-vie*.

There's a Spanish chorizo to suit everyone's taste, from mild to hot.

Ciruelas pasas
Prunes. Very good soaked in *anís*.

Clavo
Cloves (literally, nails).

Coca mallorquina
Close cousin to the Italian pizza, with tomato and onions and often sausage on top – cheese is less common. Sweet versions include currants or candied fruit.

Cochifrito a la navarra
Milk-fed lamb stewed almost without vegetables, just lemon juice or vinegar, garlic and paprika or saffron.

Cochinillo asado
Suckling pig, roasted when it is young and so tender it can be carved with the edge of a plate.

Cocido
'Cooked'; in Spain this really means simmered. *Cocido de col* is simply simmered cabbage.

Cocido madrileño
Meat dish of salt pork, beef and stewing hen, simmered in a pot with chickpeas. A second pot contains cabbage and *chorizo*. Sometimes *pelotas* (meat dumplings) are simmered too. The meal is served in two or three courses. First the broth (*caldo*) with rice or noodles in it as soup, often the cabbage and sliced sausage second, and then the sliced meats and chickpeas (sometimes with tomato sauce or pickles) last. Every region in Spain has its own *cocido*, often with more vegetables. For example, the Basques include red beans, while in the south it tends to be sweeter, with pumpkin or sweet potatoes – and every region includes its own local sausages.

Coco
Coconut. *Cocos* or *cocados* are little coconut cakes.

Cóctel
Cocktail, as in *cóctel de mariscos* (seafood cocktail).

Cogollo
Means a 'core' or 'heart'. Often means quartered lettuce hearts, but also artichoke bases and *cogollo de palmito* (palm heart).

Col
Cabbage.

Cola
Tail. *Cola de vaca* is oxtail; see *rabo de toro estofado*.

Col blanca or de Milán
White cabbage (from Milan). Served *ajiaceite*, or *rellena* (stuffed).

Coles de Brussels
Brussels sprouts.

Coliflor
Cauliflower.

Coliflor frita
Marinated cauliflower, crumbed, or egged, then fried.

Collejas
Dandelion. Cooked in omelettes with spinach, or in a dish of pig's trotter.

Colmenilla
Morel mushrooms.

Col rizada
Curly kale.

Col roja
Red cabbage.

Comino
Cumin. Introduced by the Arabs, and used in many Spanish recipes.

Compota
Cooked dried fruit.

Concha fina or almeja fina
The big Venus shell clam (*almeja*), with a mahogany-coloured shell. It is eaten raw, with chilled Fino. Inside it is a glory of scarlet and orange, hence the name 'fine shell'.

Concha peregrina
Scallop. Their shells are the badge of Santiago pilgrims; see *vieiras*.

Conejo
Rabbit; *del monte*, if it is wild. This popular food is commonly stewed (*guisado*) with onions, herbs and wine, or with cider in the north. A gravy with chocolate is also common. *Conejo al ajillo* has plenty of garlic, *capirotada* has an almond sauce. Pies and cold jellied rabbit *al vinagreta*, or *en salmorejo*, are also popular.

Conejo con caracoles
A traditional Catalan dish, a combination of snails and rabbit, both 'free food'. The snails feed on rosemary and so flavour the meat.

Congrio
Conger eel. Good with *salsa verde*; see *merluza*.

Consomé al jerez
Correctly *caldo* (broth) laced with sherry and the founder of a great tradition of clear soups.

Coques, coquetes
Flat breads; see also *coca mallorquina*.

Coquinas
Wedge shell clams. Eaten raw, or like *almejas*.

Corazón
Heart. Best stewed and often included in a lamb stew.

Cordero
Lamb. A luxury but it is eked out with vegetables when stewed.

Cordero al chilindrón
An Aragón speciality of lamb stewed with red peppers.

Cordero a lo pastor
Stewed lamb, seasoned with a little garlic and saffron and a sauce thickened with its own liver.

Cordero asado
Roast lamb. At its best from a baker's oven. The very best examples are *cordero lechal* or *mamón* (suckling lamb).

Cordero asado a la manchega
Lamb roasted in an earthenware dish with garlic and onions.

Cordonices
Wild quail. These are large and plump like French quail, not tiny

Crema catalana *makes a deliciously rich end to a meal.*

farmed birds. See also *pochas con cordonices, zurrón.*

Cordonices al ajillo

Quail, roast or pot roast with wine or garlic, often stuffed with their own gizzards.

Cordonices en hojas de parra

Quail wrapped in vine leaves.

Corvina

Sea bass or croaker. Good to eat fried, or cooked like *lubina.*

Corzo

Roe deer.

Costellada

Lamb chops grilled over an open fire with *butifarra*, a Catalan dish.

Costillar

Rack of ribs.

Costillas a la parilla

Spare ribs grilled or baked (*al horno*). Excellent with *alioli.*

Costra

Means 'crust'. So with cheese (*costrada Manchega*) it becomes toasted cheese.

Costrada

Can be a pastry slice (or *millefeuille*) with custard and fruit, or a cake with a crusty, candied top.

Costrada navarra

A layered soup of *chorizo* or bread and vegetables, soaked in broth then baked with eggs on top to make a crust. This is a common way of presenting thick soups. The same name can stand for a creamy dessert.

Crema

A puréed soup; can be sweet.

Crema catalana

Cream dessert. The custard is strongly flavoured with cinnamon and lemon zest, then fiercely grilled with a minute amount of sugar. The result is a net of caramel and a slight taste of the grill. This *crème brûlée* is served very cold.

Crema de San José

A chilled egg custard; see also *natillas*.

Cremadina or crema pastelera

A custard filling – the French *crème pâtissière*.

Cremat

Catalan for 'burnt'. It is used for their wonderful pudding and for flamed coffee. *Pescado al cremat* means fish in 'burnt garlic' sauce: that is, really cooked to a rich golden brown.

Criadillas

Pork testicles, made into fritters.

Criadillas de la tierra

Truffles; see *trufa*.

Croquetas

Deep-fried croquettes. These are a popular tapa, and are made of minced meat, bound with egg, or based on *béchamel* sauce, egged, crumbed and fried. These are also delicious made with *bacalao*, shrimps (*quisquillas*) or spinach (*espinacas*).

Cru de peix

Literally 'raw fish', a quick-cooked fish stew with saffron and paprika.

Crudo

Raw. *Para comer crudo* means 'to eat raw'.

Cuajada con miel

Junket (very like yoghurt, but made from milk curd). Sold in little straight-sided earthenware pots and eaten with honey, and also made into a cheesecake. *Cuajo* is rennet, which curdles the milk.

Culantro, cilantro

Coriander.

D

Dátiles

Palm dates – a super-sweet fresh fruit.

Delicias

Literally 'delights', it stands for a little tapa biscuit or sponge cake. See *palmeras de hojaldre*.

Dentón

Dentex (fish), a bream with pinkish tints. It makes very good eating, especially grilled or baked with onion (*al horno*). Little and lesser breams tend to end up in soup.

Despojos

Offal.

Dorada

The best and most expensive of the breams, called a gilt-head because of its golden eyebrow.

Dorada a la sal

Dorada baked completely encrusted with salt, then hammered open at the table.

Dulce

Means 'sweet', and hence is used

for sweets. Stiff cold fruit pastes such as *dulce de membrillo* (quince) are common.

Duquesa

A pie shaped like a little English pork pie; it may contain fish or vegetables. *Duquesitas* are smaller and sweet.

E

Eglefino

Haddock. Found smoked but rarely fresh.

Emborrachada

'Drunken', so meaning marinated or in wine sauce.

Embutido

A general name for sausages and cold cuts of meats, meaning literally 'stuffed'. Includes *jamon*, *chorizo*, *salchichón*, *mortadela* etc.

Empanada

Baked crust pie, usually filled with mincemeat, spinach or corn. *Empanada gallega* is a big tray-sized pie filled with tuna and tomato sauce.

Empanada de lomo

Pork loin and pepper pie, called *de raxó* in Galicia. Pies are also made of fish, such as the skinny, yellow-fleshed *xouba* and *de vieiras* (scallop pie); others are made of *bacalao*.

Empanada de Pascua

Easter pie of young lamb.

Empanadillas

Small savoury fried pies. Tuna and tomato are good and rather spicy if they are *murciana*, or they may be pork or ham with spinach. The dough is sold ready-cut in packets. The name includes sweet doughnuts, which may contain jam – *cidra*.

Empanados/...das

Means 'breaded' and then fried, for example, cutlets.

Emparedado

Sandwiched, literally 'enfolded'. Often served warm; ham or cheese in toasted bread or fried in butter.

Empedrada, la

This 'speckled' dish is a Catalan salted cod salad with broad beans.

Emperador

A variety of swordfish, slightly bigger and lacking the characteristic orange tone; see *pez espada*.

Encargo, por

Made to order.

Endibia

Endive.

Enebro

Juniper berry.

Eneldo

Dill.

Ensaimada

A delicious sweet yeast roll in a spiral, which is served for breakfast in Mallorca. Larger versions, the size of pizzas, may be topped with slices of red pork sausages.

Ensalada

Salad. The best-known salad is crisp lettuce, onion rings and olives, perhaps with tomato slices. However, *ensalada mixta* in a larger restaurant is likely to be an elaborate mixture of vegetables. Other possibilities are *lechuga* (lettuce), *tomate* (tomato), *de habas* (cooked beans), perhaps dressed with mint, and seasonal salad (*del tiempo*). They are accompanied by oil and vinegar, to dress yourself, and often include tuna and hard-boiled eggs. Other options replace lettuce with spinach, *canónigos* (lamb's lettuce) or Italian *rúccola*, often combined with raisins, nuts or pine nuts and goats' cheese.

Ensalada campera

Salad containing boiled potatoes, green peppers and onion, dressed with oil and vinegar.

Ensaladilla

Means 'little' or Russian salad, a mixture of cooked, diced potato with peas, carrots, hard-boiled eggs and tuna in mayonnaise.

Entrecot a la pimienta

Steak with peppercorns, *not* chopped vegetable peppers.

Entremeses variados

Assorted appetisers. *De carne* is a selection of sliced meats.

Erizos de mar

Hedgehog sea urchins. They are broken and eaten with a spoon like a boiled egg, combined with scrambled egg, or used for a creamy sauce.

Escabeche

Pickled by stir-frying in oil with wine or vinegar and bay leaves. Fish, meat and vegetables such as aubergines (eggplants) are all cooked this way, then left until cold. *Escabechado* literally means pickled.

Escaldums

Chicken or turkey pieces are pan-fried, then finished in an onion and tomato sauce, thickened with almonds and *sobrasada* sausage.

Escalivada

A delicious salad of cold, baked vegetables, such as aubergines (eggplants) and peppers, dressed with virgin olive oil and sometimes anchovies. The name means 'barbecued'. Tomatoes may be included too. The vegetables may also be puréed and served chilled.

Escaloña

Shallot (a kind of garlic).

Escarola

Endive (the curly and prickly lettuce).

Escorpena, escorpión

Scorpion fish, also called *rascacio*. Mostly used for fish soups, but the flesh (under the venomous spines) is good if served filleted.

Escudella i carn d'olla

The Catalan *cocido* of boiled meat. It usually includes ham,

The sweet and yeasty ensaimada – *see page 46 – is a tasty start to the day.*

chicken, cubed veal, *butifarra*, dried chickpeas or haricot beans and fresh vegetables. The broth is served first, followed by the meat and vegetable course. *Escudella de pagès* means 'country-style', with carrots, potatoes and cabbage.

Espada, pez

Swordfish. *Filetes* are good grilled. See also *pez espada*.

Espadín

A sprat; the name is also used to refer to whitebait if they are very small.

Espaldilla

Shoulder of beef or pork. Good pot-roast.

Espárragos con dos salsas

White canned asparagus with a vinaigrette, served with mayon-naise or with a sauce of chopped tomato.

Espárragos trigueros or amargueros

Wild (bitter) asparagus, which once 'grew among the wheat'. A spring speciality, best with scrambled eggs (*revueltos*), it is also sautéed or baked with crumbs.

Especias

Spices. Garlic can be considered as the king of Spanish flavouring condi-ments. Spanish spices date from Moorish times. Cinnamon (*canela*), appears in many savoury dishes. *Comino* (cumin) was liked by the Moors and is a main ingredient in the spice mix *pinchitos morunos*. Other common spices are paprika, black pepper, marjoram, thyme, bay leaves, parsley, basil and rosemary.

In specialist shops, mixtures are sold for tripe, snails, fish and for *adobos de carne* – meat marinades. Saffron or *colorante* is also sold to dye *paella* yellow.

Espetón or en espeto

Cooked on a spit.

Espinacas

Spinach. It makes soup with *garbanzos* (chickpeas) and is stewed in a mixed *menestra*.

Espinacas a la catalana

Spinach tossed in butter with pine nuts and raisins. Variations may include chard or cardoon, sometimes with chunks of ham.

Esquiexada

A Catalan starter salad of slivers of red pepper, tomato and raw salted cod.

Estofado

This does not mean stuffed, but braised. *Estofado de buey* is beef stew. It will include roots such as carrot and turnips in the northwest, and potatoes in the south. *Estofado a la catalana* may contain chocolate.

Estornino

Spanish mackerel, with pinkish oily flesh. It is of good quality, so some people prefer it to *caballa* (common mackerel).

Estragón

Tarragon.

F

Faba, fave

A large buttery-textured dried bean, typical in Aragón, Asturias and Galicia. Normally stewed with garlic and paprika.

Fabada asturiana

A famous slow-cooked bean dish in Asturias, with ham and salt pork and made spicy with saffron, *morcillas* and *chorizo*.

Fabes a la granja

Spain's top white beans: *a la granja* indicates a superior dish.

Faisán

Pheasant.

Faisán a las uvas

Pot-roasted pheasant in port, served with grapes.

Faisán al modo de Alcántara

Europe's most celebrated game dish: pheasant stuffed with its own liver and truffles. It is marinated, roasted and served with truffle and port sauce. The recipe was found in a Spanish monastery by a looting Napoleonic army and promoted by the French chef Escoffier.

Falda de ternera rellena

Stuffed flank (of veal).

Faramallas

Sweet fritter in Galicia.

Farro

This vegetable soup takes its name from pearl barley, but sometimes it contains *vermicelli* instead.

Faves, fabes

Beans; Asturian dialect for the Castilian *habas*. Used for *fabada* in Asturias, but also eaten in the south in vegetable stews such as *faves al tombet*; see *tumbet*.

Fesol

Type of dried bean.

Fiambre

Cold pressed meat (though a *fiambre de bonito* is made from tuna). *Fiambre de ternera* is veal pâté.

Fideos

Vermicelli. It is now sold in a variety of thicknesses and is a popular addition to soups.

Fideuà a la mariscos

A wonderful shellfish *paella* – but made with *fideos*, not rice.

Filete

A fillet – of beef or fish.

Filloas

Large crêpes, cooked on a griddle like the Breton versions, and jam- or custard-filled. A Galician speciality.

Flamenquines

Originally rolled-up ham and cheese, deep-fried as a tapa. The more sophisticated versions may include pork or be enclosed in *béchamel* and a crumb coating before frying.

Flan de huevos

Moulded caramel custard and Spain's national sweet, which is excellent if *casero* (home-made). *Flan de naranja* is made by adding orange juice. Other flavours include *de vanilla* or *de café*.

Flaó, flaón

Sweet cheesecake, often flavoured with *anís*. Tiny versions are pastries with curd cheese.

Flores

These 'flowers', also called *frutas de Sartén*, are sweet fritters, made with eggs, flour and milk. They may be 'flower-shaped' (*manchegas*) and are sprinkled with honey or sugar.

Frambuesas

Raspberries.

Francesa, a la

In the French style, that is, with a white sauce.

Frejol

Type of dried bean.

Fresas

Strawberries. Usually without cream. Delicious *con anís* or with Oloroso sherry.

Fricadelas

Meat patties.

Fricandó

Small pieces of beef or veal, fried, then finished in a sauce, as in French cooking.

Frijoles or frejoles

Dried kidney beans. In the Canary Islands, black beans and rice are *frijoles con arroz*.

Frío

Cold.

Fritanga

Greasy, fried food.

Frito

Fried, so *fritos* are fritters. A fried dish, *frito de cordero*, is excellent made with young lamb. *Fritillos* (little fritters) may be sweet.

Fritura de pescado

A fry-up of mixed fish; *fritura a la gaditana* or *malagueña* are deliciously crisp; see *pescaíto frito*.

Frixuelos

Sweet pancakes served with honey.

Fruta

Fruit. Some less familiar fruit worth trying, all of them half-wild in Spain, are figs (*higos*), pomegranates (*granadas*) and prickly figs (*higos chumbos*).

Frutas de Aragón

Crystallised fruits that are then chocolate-coated.

Frutos secos

Generic name for nuts and dried fruits (nuts, almonds, raisins, prunes etc.). *Frutos secos variados* is a nut and dried fruit cocktail, of which there are sweet and salted versions. There are specialised shops called *frutos secos* that also sell crisps and sweets.

Fuerte

Highly spiced, possibly with added vinegar. 'Something stronger' (*más fuerte*) means alcoholic if applied to drinks. *Fuerte* means bitter or unripe, if applied to fruit.

G

Gachas

Gruel. A survivor from medieval times, made with wheat or other flours (such as *gofio*). It can be milky and sweet (with aniseed and lemon) or flavoured with garlic and ham. In some places it is so thick that it sets when cold (like porridge) and slabs are then fried. There is a garlic and potato version made in the south.

Galets, sopa de

A typical Catalan Christmas soup. *Galets* are small pasta, and this soup also contains small meatballs. It is flavoured with celery leaves.

Galletas

Any crisp biscuits or salty crackers.

Gallina

Hen, a well-stewed chicken dish.

Gallinejas

Fried tripe from a hen or other bird, a popular tapa in Madrid's street feasts, such as San Isidro (in May) or La Paloma (Assumption, on 15 August).

Gallineta

Norway haddock (also called bluemouth and red fish) and related to rascasse. Famous for soups. Its firm flesh is good cooked like bream; see *dentón*.

Gallo

Apart from meaning 'rooster', this name also refers to a popular flatfish. It is best fried with plenty of lemon juice squeezed over.

Galludo

Dogfish or small shark. Good to eat; see *cazón*.

Gamba

One of the best prawns, sold raw in Spain, fresh or frozen. Needs 2–3 minutes' cooking in boiling water.

Gambas al ajillo

One of Spain's most popular tapas, prawns fried with garlic and parsley.

Gambas a la plancha

Grilled prawns, also highly popular.

Gambas con gabardinas

'Prawns in mackintoshes', battered then deep-fried until crisp; a popular tapa.

Gambas pil-pil

Prawns sizzling in oil and garlic, made very hot with chilli. Mop the juice up with your bread (see recipe, pages 141–2). The dish has no relation to the *bacalao* of the same name. In the south, it is sometimes called *piri-piri* after a similar Portuguese dish.

Ganso

Goose; see also *oca*.

Garbanzos

Chickpeas, the potatoes of Spain. They need soaking, then 1 to 1½ hours' simmering. The equivalent of crisps are chickpeas served *salteados*, nutty and ready-sautéed as a snack, or toasted (*torrados*). *En remojo* in a market means 'soaked'

for cooking. *Refritos* means boiled and fried in a new dish.

Garbanzos con chorizo

The perfect combination of nutty chickpeas with spicy sausage to flavour them.

Garbanzos con espinacas

A stew of chickpeas, spinach and garlic, perhaps with tomato and peppers (see recipe, page 133).

Garbure navarro

A Spanish version of a French soup, with a mixture of vegetables and salt pork, and probably *chorizo*.

Garrapiñadas

See *almendras, tostadas*.

Gatavask

Also called *gâteau basque* and *pastel vasco*, this is a heavy sweet-pastry tart, with set custard, jam or fruit inside. Excellent for picnics.

Gazpacho

The famed chilled soup is made from puréed bread and garlic, with raw peppers, tomato and cucumber, made creamy with oil and vinegar; this is labelled *andaluz*.

Gazpacho blanco

A creamy white version of *gazpacho*, based on garlic, vinegar and almonds, often *con uvas* (with Muscat grapes). See *ajo blanco*.

Gazpacho manchego

A rich mixed game pâté. The liquid is thickened with breadcrumbs, as in *gazpacho* soup, which explains the name.

Gazpachuelo

A creamy soup, served just warm, based on mayonnaise, sometimes thinned with fish soup. It may contain potatoes and their cooking water. The connection with *gazpacho* is the vinegar in it.

Gelats

Catalan for ices. Try Mallorca's *gelat d'amentilla* (almond sorbet).

Giraboix

A salted cod stew with vegetables from Valencia, including green beans and cabbage, as well as potatoes, served with *alioli*. The highly seasoned broth can be served as soup starter.

Girasol

Sunflower. Unripe black seeds are crushed to make a bland cooking oil. The white seeds are eaten as a snack.

Glorias

A little sweet pastry (sometimes a meringue) with an almond or sweet potato filling.

Gofio

Toasted cornmeal. In the Canary Islands, this is made into balls as a substitute for bread.

Golosina

A sweet titbit.

Granada

Pomegranate. The fruit is hard outside and crammed with red seeds inside. Soak it in hot water to make it easier to peel. Swallow or spit out the tiny seed enclosed in each capsule of juice, as you please. *Granadina* may be a syrup of the juice.

Granadina

Grenadine, the yellow passion fruit. Or see above.

Granizado

A grainy fruit sorbet or, sometimes, iced drink: the Spanish version of the Italian *granita*. The Catalan is *granissat*. The most common is *granizado de limón*.

Gratinado

Au gratin.

Greixera

A Mallorcan casserole. There are meat versions, and others with layered vegetable and eggs, such as *greixera d'ous*. One is like a quiche filling without the pastry. Desserts are made, too, all in the shallow round-bottomed casserole, the *greixonera*.

Greixera al llagosta

Lobster gratin, with a spinach and egg sauce.

Greixonera de brossat

A cheesecake in Mallorca, made with Requesón. Less commonly, a baked bread-and-milk pudding.

Grelos

The spring leaves and flower buds of turnip tops, stewed; see *lacón con grelos*.

Grosellas

Red- or blackcurrants.

Guinda
Cocktail or glacé cherry.

Guindilla
The one hot chilli in the Spanish kitchen, used for cooking, and sold dried as *rama*, and pickled in jars. The name means 'cherry-red'.

Guirlache
A hard toffee containing toasted almonds and aniseeds.

Guisado
Stewed. This may be a stew of vegetables alone, as in *guiso de espárragos amargueros* (stew of wild asparagus).

Guisantes
Peas. Often stewed with ham *a la española*, or tomatoes, and included in *menestra* and many veal dishes.

Guiso
Stew.

Guiso de trigo
Historic soup with wheat grains, and usually chickpeas and turnips.

H

Habas
Fresh or dried broad beans. *A la catalana* is beans cooked with *tocino* (pork fat) and *butifarra*. *Ensalada* is a bean salad that includes mint.

Habas con jamón
Fresh broad beans combined with fried ham, parsley and hard-boiled eggs. It is also called *habas españolas*. *Rondeña* and *a la granadina* will also have tomatoes and artichokes.

Habichuelas
Green summer beans or kidney beans.

Hamburguesa
Hamburgers. In Spain, they are made of minced pork, and pork and beef mixtures, as well as all beef.

Harina
Flour.

Helado
Ice-cream is sold in the usual European flavours: *de vainilla*, *de chocolate* and *de limón*, all of which you can guess. Strawberry is *de fresas*. Other unusual Spanish ices are *moscatel* (Muscat grapes) and *turrón* (nougat). Lately, more experimental ice-cream makers have come up with new flavours such as *cocido*, *tomate*, *chorizo* etc. A *copa* is a sundae, while a *tarta helada* is an ice-cream with a sponge layer. An ice-cream cone is *un cucurucho*.

Helado quemado
Ice-cream in a pot, topped with grilled sugar.

Hervido
Poached, from *hervir* (bubble, boil).

Hierba buena
The 'good herb' is mint. Its use dates back to the Arabs.

Hierba Luisa
Lemon verbena.

Higadillos, higiditos

Chicken livers. *Salteados* are sautéed, and they are much used with rice and eggs.

Higado de ternera

Calf's liver. *Con cebolla* is with fried onion and often ham. *Higado guisado* is stewed lamb's livers with onions and potatoes.

Higos

Figs.

Hinojo

Fennel. Wild in Spain, it is added to fish and used for salad.

Hogaza de pan

A thick, rounded loaf of bread, more common in rural Spain.

Hojaldre

Layered like 'leaves', and so puff pastry. The Spanish version is a bit heavy. Usually it is sweet, for example, in cream slices, but *hojaldre de salmón* is salmon pie.

Hojas de parra

Vine leaves. Served stuffed with minced meat and bread, or wrapped round birds such as quail.

Hongos

Also called *setas*, wild mushrooms that grow around tree stumps. Excellent with crêpes or eggs. Cooked with sherry or Málaga wine *a la Andaluza*. Never pick your own – buy them from the markets.

Hornazo

A 'baked' Easter cake, decorated with eggs, and sometimes containing sausage.

Stew-lovers should look for the word guiso *on the menu – this version includes skate.*

THE VERSATILE EGG

As well as the basic cooking methods, eggs are treated as a separate course in Spain. They may be added to many vegetable, pork or game mixtures, or have additions such as prawns or chopped tomato. An egg may be *pasado por agua*, boiled for 3½ minutes, enough for the white to solidify but leaving the yolk liquid, good for dipping bread. You peel it and eat it with a spoon. *Huevos estrellados* are fried 'crashed' on top of potatoes, similar to *huevos rotos* (broken eggs), while *Escalfados* are poached and *fritos* are fried or deep-fried; the latter are puffy and excellent.

Huevos a la flamenca An egg dish of many colours, hence the name. A tomato and vegetable sauce goes in a casserole, then the eggs, which may be topped with ham, *chorizo* and prawns, before baking (see recipe, page 130).

Huevos a la gitanilla Gypsy eggs, baked in a purée of bread and almonds ground with cumin, and garlic.

Huevos duros Hard-boiled eggs. Popular in *ensalada mixta* or *ensaladilla*.

Huevos rellenos Popular stuffed hard-boiled eggs, often with tuna or anchovy (*de anchoa*).

Huevos revueltos Scrambled eggs, commonly served with mushrooms.

Horno
Oven.

Hortelana
The adjective 'vegetable' from *huerta* (the 'vegetable plot'). It often indicates vegetables as a garnish, which is uncommon in Spain.

Huesos
Bones.

Huesos de santo
'Saint's bones', for All Saints. Once these were deep-fried potato pastries, stuffed with custard, but now they are little almond paste rolls filled with *cabello de angel* or marzipan.

Huevas
Fish roes. Often *aliñadas* (marinated) or *fritas*, made into crisp fritters.

Huevas prensadas
Salted pressed roe, mainly of tuna or hake, but also of many other species.

Huevo
Egg (see page 56).

I

Idiazábal, queso de
Pride of the Basque country, this hard pressed ewes' milk cheese is shaped like a small drum. Smoked versions are stronger, with toffee-coloured rinds.

Intxaursalsa
A Basque walnut cream, eaten chilled on Christmas Eve.

J

Jabalí
Boar, found in northern and southern Spain. *Estofado* (stewed) and *a la montañesa* are both with herbs and onion.

Jamón
For Spain's famous raw ham, see *serrano*. Cooked ham on the bone is called *jamón de York*. Lean slices are often called *magro*. Lesser hams are made with shoulder (*fiambre de paleta*).

Jamón al jerez
Braised ham in sherry.

Jamón con melón o higos
Sliced ham with melon or figs.

Japuta
Pomfret (fish). An excellent fish – though this name means 'son of a bitch'; see *palometa*.

Jarrete de ternera
A shin bone of veal or pork made into some tasty stews.

Jibia
Another name for cuttlefish; see also *sepia*. It is excellent served *en salsa* – in a sauce with saffron and cumin.

Judías
Dried beans. *Judías pintas* ('painted beans') are the speckled brown borlotti beans.

Judías a lo tío Lucas
A popular dish from Madrid consisting of mildly spiced beans. The Uncle Luke of the title invented it in Cádiz to feed the half-starved sailors waiting to be paid off at the end of voyages.

Judías blancas
Haricot beans.

Judías verdes
Green beans. Those *con salsa de tomate* are with tomato sauce, while *con jamón* indicates that they come with ham. They are normally the main element in *menestra de verduras*; in Madrid they are cooked along with *tocino* and *chorizo*.

Juliana, en
A way of presenting vegetables, chopped into long, thin pieces, as in *lechuga en juliana*.

Julivert
The lovely Catalan word for parsley.

Jurel
Horse mackerel (fish), related to *chicharro*.

K

Kokotxas, cocochas
Triangular throat pieces from the hake, and a Basque speciality. Delicious as tiny fritters (*fritas*), they also garnish fish dishes, but are a bit gelatinous cooked with oil and garlic as *pil-pil*.

Koskera
See *merluza a la vasca*.

L

Lacón con grelos
A hearty Galician soup-stew of cured pork shoulder with the young leaf tops and flower buds or turnips, plus new potatoes.

Lamprea
Lamprey (fish).

Langosta
The tiny-clawed rock lobster, called crawfish in Britain and crayfish in the US. Often served cold with mayonnaise; it is served hot in a spicy tomato sauce *al estilo de Bilbao,* or in rice.

Langosta a la Costa Brava
Crawfish in tomato sauce flavoured with sweet white wine and brandy, and thickened using almonds and hazelnuts.

Langosta con pollo
A Catalan mixture of lobster and chicken, in a *sofrito*-based tomato stew, thickened with a *picada*, which may contain cinnamon or chocolate.

Langostinos
Big deep-water prawns. Perhaps the best prawns, they are boiled or cooked simply *a la plancha* (on the hot iron) and served dressed *a la vinagreta* or with pungent *alioli*. They are also cooked in white wine (*a la marinera*).

Laurel, hojas de
Bay leaves.

Lebrada de progonaos
Stewed hare in wine. Like the French civet, it includes the animal's blood, but in Spain the sauce is thickened with pine nuts.

Lechal, lechazo
Milk-fed lamb. Glorious roasted.

Leche, arroz con
Cold, milky rice pudding, flavoured with lemon zest. A speciality in the northwest. Sometimes it has a grilled sugar and cinnamon topping (*quemado*).

Leche condensada
Condensed milk.

Leche frita
Literally 'fried milk', these hot or cold squares of stiff custard are creamy inside, with a crisp crust from being egg-and-crumbed, then fried. Found in the north.

Lechecillas de ternera
Calves' sweetbreads. Popularly made into a stew that may also include the liver and lights.

Lechón asado
Roast suckling pig.

Lechuga
Lettuce. Usually a salad, but also cooked. *Cogollos* (hearts) may be floured and fried, and are sometimes mixed with other hot vegetables. *Lechuga romana* is the long, dark green lettuce.

Legumbres
Pulses, fresh or dried.

Lengua
Tongue in the singular will be an ox tongue; in the plural, it refers to lambs' tongues.

Lengua estofada
Braised tongue with vegetables, served hot. In Mallorca, pomegranate juice may also be included.

Lenguado
Sole, small and big. It is stewed, baked or coated with flour or crumbs, for example, *a la gaditana*. In Madrid and the Basque country, it is often paired with wine and mushrooms or with clams and ham; in Andalucía, where tiny single-person fish called *acedías* are common, it is served with tomatoes and peppers.

Lentejas
Lentils. They are made into soups (*sopa*) or stewed (*cocido*). The stew contains potatoes, courgettes, *chorizo* or *morcilla*. *A la zamorana*, they are cooked with *morcilla*, garlic and paprika.

Many hearty Spanish stews are made with lentils.

Levadura

Both baking powder (*en polvo*) and yeast (*fresca*).

Liadillos

'Tied up', and so stuffed meat or cabbage rolls.

Liebre

Hare. Mostly served *guisada* or *en su salsa* (stewed with herbs). Red wine is a common addition, with nutmeg, and the sauce is thickened with the liver.

Lija

A small shark; see *pintarroja* or *cazón*.

Lima

Lime.

Limanda

Lemon sole.

Limón

Lemon.

Lisa

Grey mullet, considered by the Spanish to be the best grey mullet Eat it grilled or baked, for it is fairly oily, but it has a good flavour and is easy to bone. It is often cooked like *lubina* or hake, and is excellent with saffron sauce (*en amarillo*), on the south coast.

Liscos

Bacon strips.

Llagosta a la catalana

A Catalan lobster dish with a sauce of peppers, tomato, wine and brandy. Sometimes it includes chocolate and almonds.

Llampuga

Catalan for *dorada*.

Llauna, a la

Catalan for 'in a metal oven dish', or baked. Usually *bacalau a la llauna* or *caracoles a la llauna*.

Llegumet

A thick dish of potatoes, beans and rice; in Alicante it includes snails.

Locha

Small cod or loach.

Lombarda

Red cabbage. Cooked *a San Isidro* is with bacon and potatoes, or with apples and wine.

Lomo

Loin. Notably pork loin, much eaten in Spain. It may be pot-roasted with sherry or sweet Málaga wine, or stuffed (*relleno*) with nuts, ham or *sobrasada* sausage.

Lomo adobado

Seasoned pork loin.

Lomo bajo

Sirloin or loin of beef.

Lomo curado

Cured pork loin.

Lomo de cerdo a la zaragozana

Pork loin cooked with ham, onions, wine, tomatoes and black olives.

Lomo de cerdo con leche

Pork loin pot-roast in milk.

Lomo embuchado

Smoked, pink pork loin cured whole in a sausage casing. It tastes like good ham. *Caña de lomo* is also a cured loin.

Longaniza

A sausage, remarkable for its length, sometimes fresh. Also a rather bland, hard, thin salami sausage, which hangs in a hank, wrapped around a wooden rod.

Loncha

Thick slice (of ham, cheese etc.).

Lubina

Sea bass. One of the finest fish, best when line-caught. Baked *Costa Brava* style with red wine and onions, poached or grilled, it is exceptional. *A la asturiana* it is cooked in brandy (or white wine) with clams or mussels and possibly potatoes. *A la sidra* is cooked in cider; *a la aragonese* is cooked with cider and apples. In Valencia it is also baked *a la sal*, or plain in salt.

Lubina Albufera

From the great Valencian freshwater lake, this sea bass is served with ground almond and paprika sauce.

Lucio

Pike.

M

Macarrones

Macaroni. Served with cheese sauce, and also chicken giblet dressing or tomato sauce.

Macedonia de frutas

Fruit salad.

Machacón

Boiled potatoes dressed with chopped tomato and pepper, boiled egg and garlic, plus oil and usually cumin.

Macis

Mace (part of nutmeg).

Maduro

Ripe.

Magdalenas

Sponge cup cakes, from the French *madeleines*.

Magro

'Lean', usually pork. *Magro con tomate* is fried ham in tomato sauce. It is also served in a sweet sauce of Málaga wine, or with cherries.

Mahón, queso de

A well-regarded, flattish square cheese, semi-hard with a tangy taste. It is made from cows' milk in Menorca.

Mahonesa, mayonesa

Two words for mayonnaise; the first reflects the belief that it was invented at Mahón (Maó), Menorca.

Maiz

Maize or sweetcorn.

Málaga, queso de

A goats' milk cheese, matured for just five days.

Mamia

Basque junket; see *cuajada*.

Manchego, queso

Spain's Cheddar cheese. Made from ewes' milk, it is sold at various stages from semi-hard, when it is mild, to *añejo* (aged) which is sharp, hard and reminiscent of Parmesan. The waxed rind bears the mark of the rope mould and the black drum form is best known, though some rinds are yellowish; colour does not indicate age.

Mandarina
Tangerine.

Manos de cerdo, manitas
Trotters. They are cooked until the fat jellies, with beans or chickpeas (*con judías o garbazos*) to absorb the fat. For *manitas rehogadas*, they are boned out and stuffed, then egged, crumbed and fried.

Mansarón
St-George's mushroom, an early spring variety. It is known as *moixerno* in Catalan.

Manteca colorá
In Andalucía, paprika-flavoured pork fat. A bread spread that may also include shreds of meat, like French *rillettes*; a good starter.

Mantecados
Rich, crumbly little 'lardy cakes' that may include ground almonds.Those from Astorga, León, are famous.

Mantequilla
Butter.

Manzana
Apple.

Manzanas asadas
Baked apples or *rellenas* (stuffed); good if the stuffing is chestnut.

Manzanillas
Common small green olives.

Mar y tierra/mar y montana
Dishes that combine the fish from the 'sea' with chicken from the 'mountain'. The most glamorous version of this is chicken with lobster in a saffron, hazelnut and chocolate sauce.

Maragota
Wrasse (fish). With coarse and somewhat insipid flesh, it is mainly used in soups. It may also be stuffed and baked (*al horno*).

Margarina
Margarine.

Mariscos
Shellfish.

Marmitako
Basque ship-board stew, which takes its name from the cooking pot (the French *marmite*). It is made from *bonito* (white tuna) and whole new potatoes in a piquant sauce.

Marrajo
Porbeagle shark. Good grilled; see *cailón*

Marrón glacés
Much more sugary than the crystal-lised French chestnuts.

Maruca or abadejo
Spanish ling, the largest member of the cod family, similar to *rosada*. It cooks more like whiting, so needs pepping up.

Masa
Bread dough or pastry.

Masa quebrada, pasta quebrada
Flaky pastry.

Mata mulo
Very fresh. Literally 'the mule killer', it refers to the speed with which fish is rushed inland.

Mataero, ajo de
A very similar dish to *morteruelo*, made with pork, bacon, liver and pine kernels.

Matalahuva/matalahuga
Aniseed (aniseed plant).

Matanza
A big event in the peasant food year, when the pig is killed by a matador, some time in November after All Saints. The sequence of dishes starts with the liver and brains on the first day, which make a splendid meal. Many sausages are made with the offal and blood.

Mató
A fresh Catalan goats' or ewes' milk cheese. There is also a creamy dessert with nuts named *mató*.

Mazapán
Marzipan. It is made into *figuritas*, which are little animals, shapes and Christmas figures.

Mejillones
Mussels. They are often included in fish sauces, soups and *paella*. They are served cold on the shell (*a la vinagreta*) or baked (*al horno*); they are also good fried in breadcrumbs (*empanados*), which have previously been stuffed (*rellenos*).

Meijillones a la marinera
Mussels opened in white wine with onion, garlic and oil.

Mejorana
Marjoram. Sweeter than oregano.

Mel i mató
Fresh cream cheese served with honey (*miel*).

Melaza
Molasses.

Melindres
'Lady-finger' biscuits, sometimes marzipan. In Galicia, they are little doughnuts covered with syrup.

Melocotón
Peach.

Melocotón en almíbar
Peaches in syrup, from Arab times.

Melocotones asados en vino tinto
Peaches baked in red wine.

Melón
Melon. Honeydews and Piel de Sapo are celebrated.

Melón con jamón
Melon with raw *serrano* ham.

Membrillo
Quince. Popular as a stewed fruit, but most of all as a stiff, sweet, pink paste, sold as *dulce*, flan or even *carne de membrillo*; good with hard cheese.

Menestra de Tuleda
Asparagus stewed with other vegetables.

Menestra de verduras
Vegetable stew, traditionally based on green beans, artichokes and carrots. At its most attractive when

it mixes boiled and fried vegetables. Chopped hard-boiled eggs are added, and ham may be included. *Menestra a la asturiana* has fried potatoes and ham, while *extremeña* is based on potatoes and greens. *Menestra de pollo* includes chicken.

Manjar blanco

This means blancmange or 'white delight' and it is a creamy ground almond dessert. It once included pounded chicken breasts. As with most almond-based desserts, its origin is related to the Arabs.

Menta

Mint.

Menudillos

Chicken giblets. Common in rice dishes, baked with eggs and in tomato sauce.

Menudos

Offal.

Menudos gitanos

Gypsy tripe, cooked with ham, chickpeas, garlic, saffron and cumin, also called *callos a la andaluza*.

Merengues

Meringues.

Merlango

Haddock.

Merlano

Whiting. A light, white rather tasteless fish, similar to *pescadilla*.

Merlo

Wrasse (fish). Used in soup.

Merluza

Hake. Spain's most popular and plentiful fish: fine-flavoured and flaky. It is cooked in cider (*a la sidra*), with capers (*alcaparras*), with potatoes (*gallega*) and is good cold (*con mayonesa*) or in batter (*rebozada*).

Merluza a la vasca

Hake with white wine sauce, clams and prawns and sometimes asparagus tips or eggs (see recipe, pages 137–8).

Merluza en salsa verde

Hake in a sauce made green with parsley. It has an onion base and contains clams, prawns and *kokotxas*. It is also called *merluza bilbaína* and *cazuela Santander*.

Mermelada

A thick, compote-like jam of any flavour. Try peach or plum jam; berries are less good. Marmalade is *mermelada de naranja*.

Mero

Grouper (fish). One of Spain's most delicious fish, it is lean and flaky. A versatile ingredient, it is good *al horno*, baked with white wine and potatoes, grilled, or served hot in orange sauce, and cold, *a la vinagreta*.

Michirones

Broad beans stewed with *chorizo* and chilli in Murcia.

Miel

Honey. Best from one flower, such as orange flower (*miel de azahar*).

Mielga

Spur dog shark. One of the best edible sharks; see *cailón*.

Mielsobre hojuelas

A traditional dessert in central Spain – flat, aniseed-flavoured fritters covered with honey.

Migas

Fried breadcrumbs or small *croûtons*. They give texture to many egg, bacon and vegetable dishes and make a dessert with chocolate sauce or grapes.

Migas canas

A savoury bread pudding of *migas* with milk, and often bacon.

Mijo

Millet.

Modroño

Arbutus. The fruit of the strawberry tree, pretty but not that good to eat.

Moixernó

Catalan name for *seta de San Jorge* (St-George's) or *mansarón*, a spring mushroom.

Mojama

The dark, salted back of the blue fin tuna. It is a luxury.

Mojarra

The two-banded bream. Excellent grilled or baked; see *dentón*.

Moje or mojete

The sauce of any stew.

Mojete

A simple salad of strips of cold roasted onions and peppers, dressed with lemon juice, garlic and oil, and sometimes cumin. Salted cod or sardines may also be included. It is eaten with bread, not

Honey and honey products on sale in a store in Barcelona.

forks. The name comes from *mojar*, meaning to 'wet' or 'dip' the bread.

Mojo colorado or mojo picón

A cold emulsion of paprika and cumin with chilli, oil and vinegar. Often served with hot fish in the Canary Islands.

Mollejas

Sweetbreads. Often stewed in wine with onion and ham.

Mollete

A soft, rounded, tender bread loaf, toasted for breakfast in Andalucía.

Mongetes, monjetes

Dried white beans served with *butifarra*.

Montadito

A small *baguette*-bun sandwich, served as a snack.

Montañesa, a la

From Santander, where the surrounding green region is known as 'the Mountain'.

Mora

Mulberry (*de morera*), or blackberry (*de zarza or zarzamora*).

Moraga de sardinas

A 'bundle' of fresh sardines, which are casseroled to good effect with olive oil, wine, garlic, lemon and parsley.

Morago

Pork loin, which is cooked over live coals in La Rioja, during the *matanza* season.

Morcilla

A black sausage including rice or onions, pigs' blood and often oregano. There are many varieties, the most famous of which come from Burgos (rice-based), León (onion-based) and Asturias (used a lot in stews such as *fabada*). There is also a sweet *morcilla dulce*, which is sliced and eaten for tapas.

Morcón

Ham made from the shoulder or other pork offcuts, well spiced.

Morena

The pleasant white flesh of the Moray eel. It is often found in fish stews; see *caldereta*.

Moreno

A small shaped almond meringue, which is twice baked.

Moreno or morena azúcar

Brown sugar.

Moros y cristianos

A dish of black beans and white rice, commemorating a medieval conflict between the Moors and Christians.

Morro

Nose and mouth. Usually pork. Often stewed with beans. Calves' cheek is a rarity, usually braised.

Mortero

A mortar, as used to crush garlic cloves.

Morteruelo

A hot hash of mixed meats including game and pounded liver, or a cold terrine with breadcrumbs, spiced with cumin.

Mostachones
S-shaped biscuits, made from an almond, sugar and cinnamon paste, which combine in pairs to make a 'moustache'.

Mostaza
Mustard.

Mucerón de primavera
Also known as *seta de San Jorge* (St-George's), a spring variety of mushroom.

Mujol, múgil
The lesser grey mullet. It is cooked in a similar way to *lisa*, but is famous for its cured roe.

Muslos
Usually chicken legs. Also Catalan for mussel.

Musola
The smooth-hound, a good-to-eat shark; see *cazón*.

N

Nabo
Turnips, *naps* in Catalan.

Napolitana
A chocolate- or cream custard-filled baked pastry.

Naranja
Orange. Excellent with raw onions as a starter (*ensalada de naranja*). *Naranjas acaramelizadas* is a salad in caramel syrup. Oranges make a delicious sorbet (*sorbete*).

Nata
Cream. Uncommon in the south, and kept for desserts, such as whipped cows' cream flavoured with cinnamon, sugar and lemon, or with nuts or fruit.

Natillas
Rich custards made with many egg yolks, cinnamon and lemon zest. These are excellent when eaten very cold. Sometimes egg whites are served as accompanying meringues.

Navajas
Long, brown razorshell clams. Eaten raw or steamed.

Nécoras
Small shore crabs. Served boiled or in soups.

Niscalo
The 'bleeding' or saffron milk cap. Spain's most picked wild mushroom; see also *rovellón*.

Níspero
Medlar. A plum-sized Easter fruit that has a double-seed, deep-yellow, grainy, sweet flesh and toughish skin.

Ñora
A sweet mild chilli from Murcia; see *romesco, salsa*.

Nuez
Nut. Commonly means walnut, as in *sopa de nueces* (walnut cream soup), from the walnut tree (*nogal*). *Nueces variadas* (or *frutos secos variados*) are mixed unshelled nuts.

Nuez moscada
Nutmeg.

O

Oca
Young goose.
Oca con peras
A gosling cooked with pears.
Olla
The cooking pot; see also *puchero*. *Olla gitana*, a 'Gypsy pot', includes any vegetable, with fruit, such as pears. *Olleta* is another vegetable pot; in Valencia it may include game.
Olla podrida
Literally means 'rotten pot', but originally comes from *poderida* (powerful), due to its richness. Typical in Burgos, but it has versions all over Castile. It is based on kidney beans and pork.
Orégano
Oregano.
Orejas
Pigs' ears. Often salted and popular eaten fried or with beans.
Orejones
Dried apricots. They are strung up in a ring, hence the name 'ears'.
Orelletes
'Little ears' (also called *orejas de carneval* – carnival ears) of twisted *anís*-flavoured pastry, deep-fried, and served with sugar or honey. A speciality from Galicia.
Oropesa
A hard, ewes' milk, Castilian cheese, stored in olive oil.

Ortiga
Stinging nettle, usually in a soup.
Ostra
The true oyster. *Ostión* or *ostrón* is the cheaper, cultivated so-called Portuguese oyster, a speciality found mostly around Cádiz. It is excellent coated and fried (*fritas*) in a *tartera*, with garlic and bread-crumbs, or served in *sopa del cuarto de hora*.
Ous
Catalan for egg.

P

Pa d'ous
Catalan for *flan* (custard dessert).
Paella a la valenciana
The original *paella*, made from saffron rice on a base of stir-fried ground *ñora* pepper and *garrafons* (haricot beans), with a mixture of chicken or rabbit, fish, prawns and shellfish, with peppers. There are many versions to be tried, and the shellfish *paella de mariscos* and a vegetable version are also popular in Valencia. *A la catalana* includes sausage, pork and peppers.
Paella al estilo de Parellada
Named after Juli Parellada, a 19th-century dandy, who asked for his 'without bones or shells' in.
Pagès
In Cataluña, meaning 'from the countryside'. *Pan de pagès* is very

solid bread.

Pagel

Sea bream; see *pargo*.

Pajaritos

Small birds. These are eaten less now that people are better off.

Paletilla

Shoulder. Used for old-fashioned dishes, such as stewed mutton (*de carnero*).

Paletilla curada (serrana)

Cured ham made from pork shoulder. Slightly smaller and cheaper than proper pork-leg ham.

Palillos

A toothpick and anything on it, usually a tapa.

Palmeras de hojaldre

A delicious biscuit consisting of two whirls of puff pastry cut side up – the French *palmiers*.

Palmito, ensalada de

Palm heart salad. It is usually served with pink mayonnaise and lettuce.

Paloma

Dove or pigeon, *torcaz* if wild; see *pichón*.

Palometa

A deep-water fish, also called *japuta*, *castañola* and *zapatero*. *Palometa negra* is pomfret (Ray's bream), excellent to eat. The flesh is faintly pink and flakes in long strands like skate. It is good fried and worthy of rich sauces. *Palometa blanca* is *pompano*.

Palomitas

Popcorn.

Pan

White bread, of excellent quality in Spain. Catalunya has a three-cornered loaf – which the Surrealist artist Salvador Dalí stuck all over the outside of his house! Wholemeal bread is *pan integral*. *Pan rallado* is breadcrumbs.

Pan de centeno

Rye bread, made in Galicia.

Pan de higos

Sweetmeat of dried figs, in a flat cake similar to the Italian *panforte*. It is coated underneath with chocolate.

Pan de pernil

Jellied ham.

Panadés

Easter lamb pies in Mallorca.

Panadons

Catalan word for pasties. They may have spinach or fish, such as tuna, in them.

Panceta

Pork belly with some lean meat – unlike *tocino*.

Panecicos

Sweet puff made of breadcrumbs with egg white, fried then soaked in syrup.

Panecillos

Bread rolls.

Panellets

Small sweet cakes. Made of almond paste, but sometimes

Papas arrugadas *uses seawater to achieve the 'wrinkles' of the title.*

sweet potato, and topped with pine nuts or almonds. They are made for All Saints' Day in many flavours.

Panquemado

'Burnt bread', a sugar-glazed breakfast bread.

Pan tomaca

Served at most Catalan meals, this is toast with tomato juice squeezed over it. Olive oil finishes it off and sometimes *serrano* and cheese are put on top.

Papas arrugadas

Meaning 'wrinkled potatoes', these are new potatoes that are boiled in seawater until salt-crusted, then baked and served with a spicy *mojo* sauce. *Papas* is 'potato' in the Canary Islands.

Papas con choco

Delicious cuttlefish and potato dish, a speciality of western Andalucía.

Pargo

Sea bream with rosy tints to its side and tail. Excellent as steaks, or stuffed or baked.

Parrilla, a la

From the grill.

Parrillada de pescado

A mixed grill of fish. In Catalunya this may include shellfish too. (*Parrillada* following a noun indicates a *gratín*.)

Pasas

Dried fruit, usually raisins; famous when from Málaga. *Pasas de corinto* are currants, while *ciruelas pasas* are prunes.

Pasiego, queso de

A fresh soft cows' milk cheese, made into cheesecake in Santander; used to make *quesada*.

Pasta
Pasta dishes.

Pasta (masa) quebrada
Flaky pastry.

Pastas
Biscuits.

Pastel
Embraces even more food than the American use of 'pie'. In most of Spain it is the word for a pastry-topped pie. *Pastel de conejo* is rabbit pie and *pastel de pescado* fish pie. It is the word for cake, and for any solid, cooked pudding.

Pastel de berenjenas
An aubergine (eggplant) pie.

Pastel de pasas
A rather soggy breadcrumb and raisin pudding. The similar *pastel de Pascua* (Easter pudding) in Mallorca is made with eggs and biscuit crumbs.

Pasteles de carne
Pasties enclosing savoury meat, perhaps with chopped egg (to absorb juice) and vegetables. *Pastel murciano* is a spicy version. They are also potato cakes including chopped sausage.

Pastellito de Crema
Cream-filled puff (also *petisú*).

Pastelvasco
See *gatavask*.

Pastillas
Pastilles (sweets). The milk-and-coffee caramels of Logroño are well-known.

Pata
Foot. *Patas de cerdo a la parrilla* are grilled trotters.

Patacu
A casserole of cabbage, haricot beans and pork ribs with potato.

Patatas
Potato. Diced potatoes are 'hazel-nutted' (*avellanada*).

Patatas alioli
One of Spain's most popular tapas. See *alioli* sauce.

Patatas a la riojana
Potatoes flavoured (and coloured) with *chorizo*.

Patatas bravas
A popular tapa of potatoes in a spicy tomato sauce – very spicy in Barcelona.

Patatas castellanas
Potatoes fried with plenty of paprika.

Patatas con huevos estrellados
French fries with 'broken' eggs on top.

Patatas pobres
'Poor man's potatoes', with garlic, peppers and parsley.

Patatas viudas
'Widow's potatoes' with only fried onion and paprika.

Paté de hígado
Liver pâté.

Pâté en lata
Canned pâté.

Pato
Duck. Commonly roasted, it is

served in the north with turnips (*con nabos*) and in Catalunya with figs, *pato con higos*.

Pato a la sevillana
A duck stew that contains vegetables, olives, sherry and, sometimes, orange.

Pato a la naranja
Duck stew, which does not taste of orange. The acidity of the bitter fruit, plus olives, cuts through the fat of the pot-roast bird. *Pato con aceitunas* (duck with olives) is baked in the oven.

Pavías de pescado
Fish fingers; see *soldaditos de Pavía*.

Pavo
Turkey. The birds are smaller in Spain and you may find breasts or roast birds stuffed with apples or with chestnuts.

Pavo solo
Cold cooked turkey breast.

Pebre, en, all-i-pebre
In 'pepper', ie paprika. This simple 'oil and pepper' sauce is good for eels (*anguilas*), fish and chicken.

Pecho de cerdo
Chest of pork.

Pechuga de pollo
Chicken breast. These may be stuffed (*rellena*) or crumbed (*empanada*) and are excellent with orange sauce (*en salsa de naranja*).

Pejesapo, pixin
Monkfish; see *rape*.

Pelotas, pilotas
Small meatballs, poached in broth like dumplings.

Pencas
Usually the stalks of *acelga* (Swiss chard), without the leaf.

Pepino
Cucumber. Mainly used as a plain salad and in *gazpacho*. *Pepinillos* are pickled gherkins.

Pepitas
Seeds in fruit.

Pepitoria de gallina (or de pollo)
A *fricassée* of hen or chicken with a distinctive Arab ground almond and garlic sauce.

Peras
Pears.

Peras al horno/al vino tinto
Pears baked with red wine and cinnamon.

Perca
Perch.

Percebes
A very expensive shellfish, a speciality of Galicia, usually translated as a 'goose-neck barnacle'. It looks like a miniature bear's claw with white fingernails, and tastes of the sea.

Perdices a la capellán
The 'chaplain's partridges' are not birds at all, but beef rolls with ham and *sobrasada* (a type of sausage) inside.

Perdiz, perdices, perdigones, perdiú
Partridge (see box, page 75).

Perejil

Parsley. In Spain it is flat-leaved and mild. It garnishes salads and goes into a *picada* and an *aliño*. Also used a lot with garlic.

Pericana

A salted cod salad that includes crumbled pieces of fried, dried red peppers, in Valencia. In Alicante and Murcia, peppers are replaced with *ñoras*, a local small and mild chilli. It is served with *coca*.

Pernil

The Catalan word for *serrano* (meaning 'leg').

Perol

A deep frying pan, used for soupy rice dishes.

Perros y gatos

'Dogs and cats' – ugly fish sold under a pet name.

Perruna

See *torta perruna*.

Perruñillas, perruñas

Sweet, cinnamon 'dog biscuits'. They develop deep cracks as they bake. *Perruñas* are richer, flavoured with lemon zest and coated with egg white and sugar.

Pescadilla

The small silver hake (sometimes called whiting). This fish is less flat than many others, with fillets on top of the backbone, so it is served belly down. Larger examples are deep-fried in a ring, with the tail in the mouth (*se come su cola*).

Smaller varieties are used to make soup; see *caldillo*.

Pescado

Fish.

Pescaíto frito

Fried fish. Usually a dish of assorted seasoned and floured fish (hake, *pijotas*, anchovies, plaice, sardines, whitebait) and shellfish (cuttlefish of several kinds). It is a star tapa, or *ración*, in Andalucía, especially on the coast.

Pestiños, pistines

A sweet fritter of *anís* or wine pastry, made by overlapping the opposite corners of a square. Deep-fried until they puff up, they are soaked in syrup and served with sugar or honey.

Petisú

A cream-filled puff, similar to *pastelillo de crema*.

Pez ángel

Angelfish shark; see *angelote*.

Pez espada

Swordfish. The flesh is firm and with a slight orange tone, almost meaty and consequently expensive; steaks are grilled, though they can be a little dry. It may be cooked like *atún*. Typical dishes are *a la cardobesa*, which is fried with a tomato sauce, or *en salsa verde*, in a green sauce traditional in the Basque country.

Pez limón

Amberjack, the fish with a long

yellow streak. It is good grilled, baked, or as fried fillets served in a sauce.

Pez martillo

Hammerhead shark. Small varieties make good eating.

Picada

The ingredients added to a sauce that thicken it. In Catalunya the *picada* is made of garlic, bread and toasted nuts.

Picadillo

'Chopped small', usually indicating minced meat. *Picadillos* is a hash, and includes sausage when used for stuffing.

Picadillo

In Andalucía, a chopped vegetable salad. See *piriñaca*.

Picante

Spicy hot. *Guindilla* is the only Spanish chilli to fear, and sometimes *pimientos de padrón* (see box, page 76).

Picatostes

Fried bread fingers or buttered toast, often sugared.

Picotas

Big plump cherries.

Pichón

Pigeon or squab. Probably pot-roasted with a little wine.

Pichón con pasas y piñones

Pigeon with raisins and pine nuts in a sherry or sweet wine sauce.

Picón, queso de

A creamy blue cheese, named after its home in the Picos de Europa.

Pierna

Meaning leg, often roasted. Lamb is *de cordero*; *a la oransana* it is cooked on top of haricot beans, like the French *boulangère*. Roast kid leg (*pierna de cabrito*) is also delicious.

Pies

Feet; see *pata*.

Pijama

Indicating the best dessert in the house: a flan and an ice, or two sorts of ice-cream, with three types of canned fruit is typical. It used to mean 'covered in whipped cream', and this is where the 'pyjamas' (formerly nightshirts) came in.

Pijotas

Baby hake. These are crisp-fried on the south coast.

Pilongas, castañas

Dried chestnuts. Made into a puréed soup or stewed with beans and pork.

Pil-pilando

A sizzling dish; see *gambas pil-pil*. One of the rare dishes served extremely hot, for Spanish food is often just warm. It has no connection with the white Basque sauce called *pil-pil*.

Pimentón

Paprika, a basic pepper in Spain.

Pimienta

Black pepper.

Pimientos
Peppers (see box, page 76).

Piña
Pineapple.

Pinchitos morunos
Small pork kebabs, flavoured with cumin and coriander.

Pinchos
Any food that can be skewered on a cocktail stick. In the Basque country, especially in San Sebastián, *pintxos* are any kind of *canapé*, similar to tapas.

Piñonatas
Expensive, rich-tasting little pine nut cakes.

Piñones
Pine nuts. Tiny and cream-coloured, they are extracted from the cones of stone pines, and are consequently expensive. The flavour is astringent, yet rich, and is much liked for sauces, vegetable dishes and cakes.

Pintada
Guinea fowl. Mainly served roasted in smart restaurants.

Pintarroja
A dogfish or small shark, also called *lija*. Good to eat; see *cazón*.

Pipas
Snack seeds. White sunflower seeds (*de girasol*) are a common snack, but pumpkin (*pipas de calabaza*) and melon seeds are also sold, often in mixed packets with salted peanuts and sweetcorn.

Piperrada
Piperra is the Basque word for 'pepper', and dishes containing them; *piperrada* is a kind of soaked pepper salad used to accompany meat or fish dishes, often containing egg.

RUSTIC PARTRIDGE
Partridge is a familiar dish for country folk all over Spain. Usually pot-roasted with a little wine, it is also good *amb rovellon* (with wild mushrooms) or in an almond sauce.

Escabeche de perdices
Partridges cooked in wine and a lot of vinegar, then chilled until the liquid turns to jelly. Rabbit, *conejo en escabeche*, is also good.

Perdices al chocolate Partridges with chocolate. Found all over Spain; not sweet at all, but with a rich, dark gravy.

Perdices a lo torero Bull-fighters are well fed and these partridges are braised with ham, tomatoes, wine and anchovies.

Perdices con coles Partridges rolled in cabbage leaves.

PEPPERS – SWEET OR SPICY

Peppers (*pimientos*) appear in many local dishes, but are also eaten on their own stuffed with lots of interesting ingredients.

Ñora A small, slightly spicy red pepper from Murcia. A part of the base of *paella*.

Pimientoas choricero Long, slim red peppers, usually dried and used in stews such as *salsa vizcaina* or *patatas a la riojana*. A saying goes, 'don't swap *choriceros* with *ñoras*'.

Pimientos de piquillo rellenos de bacalao A Basque speciality of spicy, long red peppers, stuffed with salted cod, then fried and served in a sauce.

Pimientos fritos Small, deep-fried green peppers. Popular all over Spain, the best are from Padrón, a town in Galicia. The famous saying warns you '*unas pican y otros non*' (some are hot, others not).

Pimientos rellenos Stuffed peppers. Usually the familiar fat versions, with ham or pork.

Pimientos rojos asados Roast, skinned red peppers, served as a salad with oil; very Spanish!

Pipirrana

A salad of peppers, tomato, cucumber and onion. Served very cold, it is close to *gazpacho*. It may contain *bacalao* or tuna, with a dressing based on hard egg yolks; it is typically served in Jaén with *serrano*.

Piriñaca

A salad of mixed chopped vegetables but without cucumber. It is typical of Cádiz, but can have other names, such as *picadillo* in Seville. The same mixture often accompanies baked fish, such as *besugo asado con piriñaca*.

Pisto

A tomato, aubergine (eggplant) and mixed vegetable sauce, meaning a 'hotchpotch'. *Pisto manchego* includes scrambled egg. Good with fish too (*pisto de peces*; see pisto manchego recipe, page 140).

Pistola

Literally, 'pistol'. A loaf of bread, like the French *baguette* but thicker. It is bought daily by Spaniards.

Pixin, pejesapo

Monkfish; see *rape*.

Plancha, a la

On the hot iron (griddle): a way of grilling with very little oil.

Plátanos
Bananas.

Plátanos fritos
Fried bananas. Popular in the Canary Islands.

Platija
Flounder (fish); the name means 'flat'. Good to eat.

Platos fríos
Cold dishes.

Pochas
Haricot beans in La Rioja. Called *judías blancas* in the rest of Spain. Best eaten fresh.

Pochas con codornices
Fresh haricots cooked with quail. The dish opens the hunting season.

Pochas riojanas
Fresh haricots cooked with *chorizo* or lamb and bacon, which reddens the podded beans.

Pocho/a
Overripe or rotten.

Poleo
Type of mint.

Pollastre amb gambes
Catalan chicken with prawns, in a red wine and pine nut sauce.

Pollo
Chicken. *Rebozado* is coated with breadcrumbs and fried. *Al jerez* is finished with sherry and *a la granadina* also includes raw ham. *Pollo con aceitunas* is stewed gently with green olives. *Pollo en arroz* (chicken in rice) is common on the north coast; see *campurriano*.

Pollo al chilindrón
Chicken cooked with peppers, tomatoes and onions. *Pollo en chanfaina* is similar; see *samfaina*.

Pollo asado
Spanish chickens are often roasted with pork fat, salt and paprika, making the skin wonderfully tasty. Also good roasted *con salsa de naranja* (basted with orange juice).

Polvorones
'Crumble cakes'. As crumbling is what these little cakes do very easily, they are paper-wrapped. The best examples include ground almonds as well as flour and sugar, flavoured with *anís* and cinnamon. They are made all over Spain, but those from Antequera are outstanding. Accompany them with a glass of *anís* or Oloroso sherry. You are advised to crush them in your hand before unwrapping.

Pomelo
Grapefruit.

Porcella asado
Roast suckling pig in Mallorca.

Porra antequerana
Very thick *gazpacho* with raw ham.

Porras
A sugared, fried dough. See *churros*.

Postre
Like the English 'afters', this also means dessert.

Postre de músico
A Christmas dish of nuts and dried

fruits, which is typically found in Catalunya.

Potaje

A thick vegetable soup – pottage – generally with chickpeas or haricot beans. Similar to *cocido*. *Potaje valenciano* has chickpeas and spinach; *potaje murciano* has rice, *habichuelas* and *frijoles* (dried beans).

Pote asturiana

A thick soup of beans and sausage. *Pote granadina* contains tomato, peppers and onions, probably with saffron.

Poti poti

Salted cod salad, with potatoes and peppers.

Pringadas

Toasted bread with melted bacon or fat spread on top. Usually it is made using the leftovers from *cocido*. The name comes from a verb that means 'to splash or wet in fat or oil'. In southern Spain, *monta-ditos de pringa* are popular small sandwiches filled with leftovers from a *puchero*.

Puchero

An earthenware cooking pot, and so a stew. The Andalucían *puchero* usually contains a range of vegetables and even tomato sauce, plus pork sausage and chicken, while in the Canary Isles *puchero canario* has pumpkin, sweetcorn, sweet potato, even pears.

Pudín

Like English pudding, it can take lots of forms, including anything moulded. It can mean a cold meat or fish mould or even a hot meat loaf. In Mallorca, it is a cold egg and bread pudding.

Puerro

Leek.

Pulga

Meaning flea, this is a very small bun-sandwich.

Pulapeta

A slice of meat; it may be rolled with a filling.

Pulpo

Octopus. *Pulpitas* indicate baby versions, which are likely to be more tender.

Pulpo a la feria

A famous Galician dish consisting of boiled octopus served in a paprika-oil salad dressing. This is usually a salad, but it might come hot from the pot.

Puntillitas

Small squid. Fried in batter, these are served as a tapa.

Purrusalda, porrosaldo

A Basque leek and potato soup. It usually includes cooked *bacalao*.

Puzol, queso de

Fresh cows' milk cheese in Valencia, moulded with a conical indent.

Q

Quemada, or tostada
'Burnt', meaning topped with caramelised sugar. Sweet bread and ice-cream prepared this way are both good.

Quesada, quesadilla
Cheesecake.

Queso
Cheese (see box, page 80).

Queso frito
Fried cheese. Slices of cheese are egged and breadcrumbed and then fried.

Quisquilla
The common prawn.

R

Raba
A north-coast squid dish, battered and floured, then fried.

Rábano
Red radish. *Rábano picante* is the stronger horseradish.

Rabo de toro estofado
Bull's tail, slow-stewed with onions and other vegetables. In Andalucía, wine is used, or sherry (*a la jerezana*).

Ración
Meaning 'serving', this is a bigger dish than a tapa, suitable for sharing or for eating individually as a main course. In southern Spain, bars also offer '½ *ración*'.

Rana, ancas de
Frogs' legs. Served fried with garlic and parsley.

Rancho canario
A stew in the Canary Isles with chickpeas, potatoes and pasta, plus a little *chorizo* and bacon.

Rape
Monkfish. Hugely popular in Spain.

A flaó cake, a type of sweet cheesecake.

SPANISH CHEESE

There are about 100 different varieties of cows', ewes' and goats' milk cheeses in Spain, some of which mix different kinds of milk. Spanish cheese is either hard or very fresh; compared with France, Spain lacks the whole middle range of matured creamy cheeses, excepting Torta del Casar or Torta de la Serena. However, there are many unusual hand-made cheeses, mainly using unpasteurised milk. There are a few semi-hard cheeses, such as Cantabria, but it is the hard cheeses that mature to distinction. Most Spanish hard cheeses pass from mild when semi-hard, to strong and sharp when hard. Some hard cheese is stored in olive oil, which allows it to mature without drying out: attractive examples are from Oropesa and those exported from Burgos by Gúzman. Creamy blue cheeses are made, much in the same style as Roquefort, for example, Cabarales.

Hard and soft cheeses bear the marks of rope moulds throughout the Manchego cheeses. The wrapping (like a Dick Whittington bundle) shows up on the Levantine Servilleta, while Puzol has a conical depression in the middle. Soft cottage and fresh cheeses are made all over the country. Spain has no long tradition of cooking with cheese – it is mostly eaten with bread before or after a meal. However, the hard cheeses grate well.

It is cooked in many ways. *A la gallega* is with potatoes and garlic. It is also fried with paprika (*en pimentón*) in the south. *Al estilo de Costa Brava*, it is stewed with tomatoes, red peppers, white wine and fresh peas. Cold, it makes an excellent salad (*ensalada*).

Rascacio, or escorpina

Rascasse (fish). It is a favourite for fish soups and stocks, but can be cooked like *dentón*.

Raspas de anchoas

Anchovy backbones, deep-fried for a tapa. It sounds terrible, but is actually crunchy and tasty.

Raya

The wingflaps of skates (the ray shark). Good to eat, as the flesh falls from the bones in attractive strips: especially good with something acid such as capers or lemon juice. It is stewed in Galicia (*caldeirada de raya*), but marinated then served *en adobo* in the south.

Raya en pimentón
Skate wings cooked with paprika.

Rebanada
Slice, eg of bread. '*Rebanar*' means to slice.

Rebañar
Rebañar means 'to wipe round the plate' – it is good manners here not to leave food on the plate.

Rebeco
Chamois.

Rebozado
Battered and deep-fried.

Recuit
A soft fresh cheese, from cows' or ewes' milk, eaten with honey or with sugar.

Redondo
Part of the beef rump, tied and roasted in a joint.

Relleno/a
Stuffed. From peppers (usually the slim, hot versions) to red cabbage to pigs' trotters, to squid; fillings are often meat and sausage.

Remojón
A *bacalao* salad; the name means 'soaked', for this is how the fish is prepared. There are several versions to try: one comes with oranges, another with peppers, potatoes, olives and-boiled eggs.

Rémol
Brill (fish). A kind of small *rodaballo*. or turbot. Cooked in a similar way.

Remolacha
Beetroot.

Reo
Sea trout, formerly called salmon trout because of its pink flesh. Cooked like *salmón*.

Repápalos
Typical in Extremadura, a kind of bread, garlic and egg croquette that can be served in a stew. Also a dessert version of bread and milk, in which little balls of egg and crumbs are fried, then served in milk and cinnamon.

Repollo
Drumhead cabbage.

Requesón
Smooth cottage cheese, often bearing pretty mould marks. In Madrid, cheeses from Miraflores and El Paular are traditional.

Revuelto con ajetes
Scrambled eggs with green garlic shoots.

Revueltos con espárragos trigueros
Scrambled eggs with wild asparagus: a springtime speciality.

Revuelto de setas
Scrambled eggs with wild mushrooms.

Revueltos
Stirred (scrambled) eggs. Unlike *tortilla*, which is a dense egg cake.

Riñonada
Kidneys in their fat, so roasted, or a kidney and other offal mix.

Riñones al jerez
Kidneys served in sherry sauce.

In poorer areas, this is made with pigs' kidneys and ham in tomato sauce. An excellent dish with veal or lambs' kidneys, and a universal tapa.

Riojana

Rioja-style. Good red peppers grow in Rioja and paprika is also made. A dish *a la Rioja* will probably contain these, or red *chorizo* sausage, which includes the paprika.

Rodaballo

Turbot. An expensive fish, cooked in many ways. *Al albarino* (in white galician wine), *a la sidra* (in cider), grilled, or baked in a cream sauce.

Rollitos

Little rolls, containing cheese, ham, meat or fish. Or sweet versions, such as *rollitos de aguardiente* and *rollets*.

Rollo de carne

Meat loaf.

Romana, a la

Any fish or shellfish battered then deep-fried. Generously, Italy is credited for something done super-latively well in Spain.

Romero

Rosemary.

Romesco de pescado

A fish or shellfish dish on the east coast, sometimes containing dried beans, to which *romesco* sauce is added before serving.

Romesco, salsa

An exceptional sauce, made of ground toasted almonds and hazelnuts, with the addition of the special sweet, mild chilli called *romesco* in the Catalan country. It is excellent with fried fish or roast chicken.

Roncal, queso de

A mild, medium-hard ewes' milk cheese, shaped like a small drum. It develops holes the size of rice. Factory-made in Navarra, it is well regarded, with most of it going to France.

Rosada

The Spanish equivalent of 'rockfish', a name for anonymous varieties of dogfish (shark) and a saltwater catfish. Always sold skinned, they are very pink-fleshed.

Roscón de Reyes

A big Twelfth Night ring yeast cake, scented with orange-flower water. The flavour and coarse texture are much like the Italian cake *panettone*. The crust is sprinkled with chopped nuts and fruit, and traditionally it has a single charm hidden in it.

Roscos

Doughnuts. Frequently flavoured with aniseed, they are made into rings and deep-fried. The most delicious examples are made in Burgos. *Rosquillas* are ring-shaped doughnuts or buns, made of batter, rich scone or even puff pastry, and usually a generous amount of egg. They are fried or baked, then sprinkled with sugar and cinnamon.

Rosquillas de Alcalá
Pastry rings, glazed twice, first with egg then sugar syrup.

Rosquillas de Santa Clara
Rings dipped in a meringue made with syrup and rebaked.

Rosquillas tontas y listas
'Clever and dim' buns, some iced with sugar, others plain.

Rossejat
A dish made with rice or thin noodles. The rice is usually paired with pork (trotters) and the noodles with fish, often hake.

Rovellón
Spain's favourite wild mushroom, it belongs to the same family as *níscalo*, which it is often called. It grows in pinewoods on mountains all over the country. Bright saffron colour, it belongs to the milkcap family, but the drops it sheds when cut are red like blood. It is usually fried with parsley and garlic, and is always expensive.

Rubio
The red gurnard. Good grilled and better baked with a sauce as it can be dry.

S

Sábalo
Shad, a freshwater fish. Often served as *escabeche* as it deteriorates fast once caught. It is also fried and served in various sauces.

Sal
Salt; *salado* is salted. Fish are baked whole in salt, which is broken open, then discarded at the table; see *dorada a la sal*.

Wild rosemary growing in Mallorca.

Salazón, en
Cured, that is, salted meat or fish
(most typically, cod).

Salchichas
Fresh sausages. Excellent braised
in sherry.

Salchichón
A good, cured, ready-to-eat sausage
– like salami. *Salchichón de Málaga*
has whole peppercorns in it.

Salema
One of the breams (fish);
see *dentón*.

Sal fina
Table salt.

Sal gruesa/gorda
Coarse salt.

Salmón
Salmon, caught in the north of the
country. Steaks (called *toros* in
Galician) are grilled, while *arroz con
salmón* is a good rice dish.

Salmón a la gallega
Galician salmon. Cooked in stock
and *aguardiente*, or white wine and
mustard, then served cold.

Salmón a la ribereña
An Asturian recipe, 'river' salmon
steaks, fried with raw ham, then
served in a simple cider sauce.

Salmón ahumado
Smoked salmon.

Salmonete
'Little salmon' are a species of
goatfish, popularly called red mullet.
Splendid grilled whole *a la parrilla*.
Tiny versions are fried and have the
most beautiful flavour. They are also
baked with lemon.

Salmorejo cordobés
Wonderful version of chilled
gazpacho. A cream of garlic bread,
tomatoes and oil, beaten to a light
emulsion, with ham and chopped
hard-boiled eggs. But beware!
Sometimes it consists of just
garlic, vinegar, oil and puréed
bread; see *ajo blanco*.

Salmuera, en
In brine.

Salpicón de mariscos
A shellfish 'cocktail' or salad; the
French term means 'chopped' ingre-
dients bound together in a sauce.
It can also be made with chicken
(*de pollo*).

Salsa
Sauce. *Salsa de tomate* includes
ketchup as well as tomatoes.

Salteado
Sautéed.

Salvia
Sage.

Sama de pluma
A bream (fish); see *dentón*.

Samfaina
One of the great Catalan sauces,
and also a vegetable dish in its own
right. It is made from aubergines
(eggplants), courgettes and peppers
in an onion and tomato sauce.

San Jacobo
A steak: Beef fillet covered with
ham and cheese then breaded.

San Pedro

St-Peter's fish has a black finger-print on either side of its big head and is extremely tasty, with four big, bone-free fillets, It is also called *pez John Dory* and cooked in the same way as *lubina*.

San Simón, queso de

A famous cows' milk cheese in Galicia, now factory-made. It is smoked and looks like a well-oiled brown pear.

Sancocho canario

A fish stew, best made of *dentón* with potatoes. In the Canary Isles, it is served with a powerful red sauce that includes chillies and vinegar; see *mojo colorado*.

Sandía

Watermelon.

Santiaguiño

The flat clawless Galician lobster. It has the cross of St-James on its head, hence the name. It is also called a *cigarra de mar* (sea cricket) because it clicks in the water.

Sardinas

Sardines. These are lovely barbecued simply on the beach. *A la santanderina* are seasoned with garlic, parsley and bread, then baked. *Moraga de sardinas a la malagueña*, also called *sardinas a la marinera*, refers to casseroled sardines with tomato sauce.

Sargo

A bream, also called *chopa*. Good grilled or baked; see *dentón*.

Sartén, de

'From the frying pan', as in *dulce de sartén* (deep-fried sweet pastries).

Seco

Dry or dried.

Sepia

Cuttlefish. Like purse-shaped squid; their flesh is sweeter but tougher. They are cooked in many ways, and used in rice dishes such as *aroz negro*, or served with potatoes.

Sepia con guisantes

A pleasant cuttlefish and pea stew.

Sequillos

Little pastries covered with meringue. Some recipes include hazelnuts or pine nuts.

Serrano, jamón

The name means 'mountain-ham', usually called simply *serrano*. Eaten thinly sliced and raw on bread, as a tapa, or chopped for cooking. The best ham is *pata negra*, from black pigs running wild. They are fed exclusively on cork-oak acorns (*bellotas*, therefore it is also called *jamón de bellota*), and are recog-nisable by the black toes of the trotter. The king of hams comes from Jabugo, north of Huelva. Others are made at Trevélez (less salty) and Montánchez. Less expensive (and leaner) hams are made from the white pig, and also from the shoulder, and called *paletilla* (so not strictly ham).

Sesos

Brains. These are often included with other meats. *Sesos huecos* – nicknamed 'scatterbrains' – are creamy light fritters.

Setas

A general term for all wild mushrooms. They are usually fried simply with garlic, wine and parsley, occasionally with ham.

Setas a la llauna

Wild mushrooms baked 'in a metal dish' in the oven with pork fat and garlic, in Catalunya.

Sidra, a la

Cooked in cider. Many fish are cooked this way on the north coast, often with potatoes, which are fried first, then soaked in the sauce.

Sobrasada

A soft, raw, red pork sausage, flavoured with paprika and with a great deal of fat. It is often served in pots as a spread, without the sausage casing; popular in Mallorca.

Sofrito

Onions fried slowly with garlic and parsley. This is one of the basics of Spanish cooking; tomato is added to make a sauce.

Soldaditos de Pavía

The original fish finger. The Spanish equivalent of bread-and-butter 'soldiers', they use fried hake or *bacalao* (cod) and commemorate the 'soldiers of General Pavía', who overthrew the first republic in 1874.

Solla

Not sole at all, but plaice. Cooked like *lenguado*.

Solomillo

Beef fillet steak, from inside the sirloin bone. It may be roasted whole and served with onion rings.

Solomillo andaluz

Pork tenderloin – an economical version of beef fillet. *A la Trianera* (named after the Seville Gypsy quarter) means roasted in sherry.

Sopa

Soup, made of the basic vegetables such as *cebolla* (onion) as well as with rice (*sopa de arroz*) and pasta (*de fideos*). *Verduras* usually includes dried beans.

Sopa aragonesa

Made of minced calf's liver, grated cheese and broth, it is finished with a crust of bread and cheese.

Sopa castellana

Garlic soup with cumin from La Mancha.

Sopa de ajo

Basically this is water thickened with bread and flavoured with garlic: it can be appalling, but has many admirers. In Ávila the bread for the *sopa de pobre* (for 'the poor') is fried first. In Rioja or Castile, it may have eggs beaten into it, and paprika.

Sopa de albóndigas

Chicken broth with veal and ham meatballs, flavoured with cinnamon.

Sopa de almendras

A sweet almond and bread soup, flavoured with cinnamon and lemon zest. It is served as a dessert in Levante at Christmas.

Sopa de cangrejos

A delicious crab bisque, made in Mallorca.

Sopa del cuarto de hora

This '15-minute' soup – quick compared to a broth – containing fried onions and rice. It may have prawns, clams and chopped ham and hard-boiled eggs in it.

Sopa de mariscos or de pescados

Shellfish soup and fish soup. Often interchangeable, but both contain both. Sometimes one fish is singled out, such as in *sopa de gambas* (prawn soup); *sopa de pescadilla* (silver hake) or *sopa de rape* (monkfish). If your finances can stretch to it, order *sopa de langosta*, lobster (crawfish) soup.

Sopa de mejillones

Mussel soup. Good in Catalunya, with tomato or white wine, garlic and *aguardiente*.

Sopa de picadillo

The name means soup with a 'chopped garnish' consisting of ham, hard-boiled eggs and fresh mint – the latter is known as a hangover cure. There are many egg and ham soups, such as *sopa alpurrañas*.

Sopa de tomate

A soup with a long history in Cádiz, made with tomatoes and red peppers.

Sopa mahimones, maimones

Arab garlic, bread and olive oil soup, sometimes with ham. It is finished in the oven to poach the eggs. Very hot and strong, it is especially good if you are tired and broke!

Sopa mallorquina

Contains tomatoes, onions, peppers, artichokes, asparagus, cabbage and other vegetables, but it is made very solid, with bread and not much liquid.

Sopas cachorreñas

A fish soup (normally cod) flavoured with pounded bitter orange zest, vinegar and oil.

Sopa torrada

A Catalan beef soup.

Sopa viña AB or de vino

Named after the Amontillado sherry from Gonzales Byass used in it.

Soplillos

Fried sweet puffs with *anís* or meringues with toasted almonds.

Sospiros de Moros

Big puffy dry meringues in Granada.

Suflé

A soufflé. Usually less good in Spain than in France.

Suizos, bollos

Breakfast rolls, slashed down the middle and baked with sugar or currants in the hollow.

**Suquet, susquet,
Suspiros de monja**

'Nun's sighs', soft meringues
poached in milk then served with
custard. Known as *oeufs à la neige*
in Britain and France and 'floating
islands' in the US.

Susquillo de pescador

A Catalan soup-stew with many
sorts of fish and shellfish, with
brandy, onions and tomatoes.

T

Tapa

Originally meaning 'lid', to describe
the famous little dishes served with
a drink (wine or beer). Tapas used
to be free, and little ones still are in
some places (for example, olives,
Russian salad, peanuts, crisps), but
today you mostly have to pay.

Tapa, tapaplana

Beef; lower rump

Tarrina, en

Little brown earthenware pots are
used for *cuajada* and soft cheese
– the Spanish equivalent of French
white ramekins.

Tarta

Usually a cake or sweet pastry.
Tartita is any small dessert,
including ice-cream in pots.

Tarta de almendras

Almond cake, often just ground
almonds, egg yolks and sugar, like
that from Puentedueme in Galicia.

Tarta de manzana

Apple tart, often of puff pastry.

Tarta de Santiago

In Santiago de Compostela on
St-James's Day, this is a pastry tart
enclosing a moist almond filling.
The topping is decorated with a
stencil of St-James's sword.

Tarta helada

An ice-cream layer cake. *Tarta al
whisky* has two different vanilla
ice-creams, a whisky sponge layer
and caramelised sugar on top.

Tarta Pasiega

A cheesecake, of fresh cheese
of the type made in the Basque
region, which is often flavoured
with *anís*.

Tejas

'Tiles'. Thin biscuits of egg white,
ground almonds and sugar, like the
French *tuiles*.

Tenca

Tench, a freshwater fish, eaten a
lot in Extremadura. Good marinated
then fried or as *escabeche*.

Ternasco asado

Baby lamb, roasted with white
wine, rosemary and thyme, a speciality in Aragón and Navarra.

Ternera

Often translated as 'veal', this is
nearer to being virgin beef, as it
can be up to two years old. *Ternera
mechada* is 'larded', for a pot-roast
or roast – it goes well with
castañas (chestnuts).

Ternera a la sevillana
Veal cooked in Montilla wine, with olives.

Ternera con alcachofas
Veal escalopes and artichoke bases cooked in a sherry or tomato sauce.

Terrina
Cold terrine or pâté.

Tetilla, queso de
A breast-shaped, soft white cow's milk cheese, now factory-made in Galicia.

Tirabeques
Mangetout or 'snow' peas.

Tocino
Pork fat, fresh or salted, cut from the belly, and almost solid fat, even though it is the same cut as streaky bacon. It is often cubed and fried to make a fine-flavoured fat (and to provide crispy bits) for cooking bean dishes. Sometimes *tocino* is fried bacon.

Tocino de cielo
A dessert of pure sweetness and texture, is served in small squares. Made from syrup and egg yolks, the name means 'heavenly bacon', because it looks like a slab of bacon, as the sugar caramelises.

Tojunto
Means 'all together'; *todo junto* is a one-pot mix of vegetables and meat.

Tomates rellenos
Stuffed tomatoes; the filling may be mince, sardines, egg salad, *béchamel* sauce or vegetables.

Tomillo, en
With thyme, a popular herb.

Torradas
Fried *torrija*, incorporated into a sweet omelette or custard.

Torrados
Toasted food.

Torreznos
Crisp, thick strips of fried pork belly.

A few tapas dishes make a delicious and informal lunch.

Torrija

A children's dessert of bread dipped in milk then fried and sugared. Like the French *pain perdu*, it is made to use up stale bread.

Torta

A flat bun or a round or oval breakfast bread topped with crunchy sugar. It can also be a tart or a cake.

Torta de aceite

Plain, flat pastry biscuits, made with oil and aniseed.

Torta de la Serena

A spectacular creamy ewes' milk cheese from Extremadura.

Torta del Casar

A rich, aromatic, Extremeño ewes' milk cheese.

Tortas de hojaldre

Cake consisting of puff pastry layers with jam.

Torta perruna

A bun eaten in Andalucía with hot chocolate.

Tortells

A breakfast bread ring with a ground almond and lemon filling. It contains potato, too – though you can't taste it.

Tortilla española

Spanish omelette. *Truita* is Catalan for *tortilla*.

Tortillitas de berenjenas

Aubergine (eggplant) fritters.

Tosta

A large *canapé* on a piece of toasted bread.

Tostadas

Literally 'toast'. This is bread only very lightly grilled to freshen it, and used to mop up sauces.

Tostadas de crema

Not toast, but breakfast fingers of cold custard, egged and breadcrumbed, then fried; very similar to *leche frita*.

Tostón

Roast suckling pig.

Toyina, or toñina

Salted tuna.

Trigo

Whole wheat, soaked. A *guiso de trigo* or *triguillo* is a soup with turnips and *acelga* stalks or squash.

Trixat

Spanish bubble and squeak. Cooked potato and cabbage, plus chopped bacon, are pressed into a mould then fried in pork fat.

Truchas

Trout. Brown trout still swim in the streams of the Pyrenees and Asturias, though restaurant versions are likely to be farmed and pink.

Truchas con almendras

Trout baked and served with fried almonds, or *con salsa de almendras*, usually a ground almond sauce.

Truchas con jamón

Ham slices are fried, then trout is fried in the ham fat and served stuffed or wrapped in ham. This is also called *truchas a la navarra*.

Trufa
Truffle. Found all over Spain but chiefly near Castellón de la Plana on the east coast.

Trumfes fadrines
Potatoes on their own, served with a little ham and egg-thickened sauce added at the last minute.

Ttoro, tioro
A Basque mixed fish stew or soup, with onion, bread and wine.

Tuétano
Bone marrow. Usually grilled slices; also known as *chamberete*.

Tumbet, tombet
A vegetable stew from Mallorca, made with tomatoes and aubergine (eggplant), it is like *ratatouille* but with potatoes added. Sometimes it is layered with meat or contains eggs.

Turrón
A Christmas speciality from Alicante, famous all over Spain. A candy-like almond nougat. *Jijona blando* is a soft coffee-coloured paste of ground toasted almonds and honey.

Txangurro, changurro
Basque for spider crab; *centollo*.

U

Urta a la roteña
A bream, related to *dentón*. Found on the southwest coast, it feeds on shellfish and so tastes of them.

Baked in a naturally sweet sauce of fried, caramelised onions.

Uvas blancas (negras)
White (black) grapes.

V

Vaca
Cow, giving beef and milk for *queso de vaca*, cheese.

Venado
Venison. A coarse meat, it is often stewed or roasted with thyme, rosemary or bay leaves, and wine.

Venado con cabrales
The best cuts of venison roasted and with a blue cheese sauce.

Veneras
Scallops.

Verduras
Green vegetables. Often served as a separate course, or included in rice or *menestra*.

Vieiras
The Galician name for scallops.

Vieiras de Santiago or Santiagüenses
Scallops in Santiago de Compostela flamed in brandy, arranged in the upper shell with tomato sauce, topped with breadcrumbs, then quickly grilled.

Vieja
The colourful parrot fish, also called 'widow' fish. Purple-backed and yellow-finned, it is very typical of the Canary Islands.

Viena, pan de
Meaning 'Vienna-style bread', a loaf of bread thicker than the French *baguette*, similar to a *pistola*.

Villalón, queso de
A soft rectangular ewes' milk cheese in Castile, sometimes shaped like a hoof.

Villeroy
A French dish, popular in Spain, of chicken breasts or prawns coated in *béchamel*, chilled then crumbed. They are fried and served hot.

Vinagre
Vinegar.

Vinagreta
Vinaigrette.

Viuda
'Widowed'. The word can apply to a meatless *potaje* and to *patatas* – and also to small, grey snails.

Vizcaína
The Spanish word for Biscay. *Salsa a la vizcaina* includes onions and dried peppers, but not tomato.

X

Xató, xatonada
Mixed dressed salad from Tarragona containing salted cod, sometimes tuna and anchovy fillets, and often tomato and olives.

Xuxos
Fried doughnuts. Nowadays served with whipped cream, originally fried round a stick, then custard-filled.

Y

Yemas
Very sweet, small yellow cakes. Named after the egg yolks used to make them and which they resemble.

Yogur
Yoghurt.

Z

Zamorana, a la
A dish of Zamora, often including black *morcilla*, onion and paprika.

Zanahoria
Carrot.

Zapata, zapatero
Means a 'shoe'/'shoemaker', also called *palometa*, but this is a fish of the bream family; see *dentón*.

Zarangollo
A hash of onion and courgettes, well-garlicked, and with fried bread.

Zarzuela
A medley of white fish with shellfish in a tomato, wine and saffron broth.

Zizak
Basque for St-George's mushroom.

Zoque
Chilled, vinegared, raw tomato and pepper soup, much like *gazpacho*.

Zorza
Fried pork with paprika, like skinless *chorizo*.

Wine and Drink of Spain

Spain produces an abundance of quality wines, and has a long tradition of grape-growing.

The Spanish climate is ideally suited to the growing of ripe, luscious grapes.

Wine and Drink of Spain

Matching its rich and varied national cuisine, Spain has a strong beverage culture, based mainly on its wine tradition. Covering a huge area of Spain, vineyards produce a wide variety of wines ranging from the more standard Bordeaux-style of northern areas to the *generoso* wines of Andalucía, what we know as 'sherry', through the young, fruity whites of Galicia, the sparkling Cavas produced mainly in Catalonia, to the young table wines of Castilla-La Mancha and the eastern Levante coast.

Spanish wine production has developed rapidly over the past 30 years. The country has become one of the biggest exporters in the world and has remained fiercely competitive due in great part to how deeply wine culture in Spain is rooted in ordinary people's daily life, as opposed to being regarded as a luxury. That is why Spain is such a great place to buy and drink wine, as you can find many bargain-priced wines, far cheaper than in France or Britain.

But that's far from being your only choice, as Spain is also a big beer producer. Spanish lager has more than 5% alcohol per volume, which makes it stronger than most European beers. It is also a major producer of brandy and liqueurs. Excellent mineral waters abound, from Vichy Catalán on the Costa Brava to Solán de Cabras from aquifers in the land of Cuenca, or Lanjarón from the springs of the Alpujarra mountains south of Granada.

Though you'll find regular breakfast tea in most shops and cafés, it is not as popular as coffee, with its wide variety of choices (*café solo*, *cortado*, *con leche*, *manchado*, etc). In summer, you can try refreshing local drinks such as tap beer, *clara*, *sangría*, *tinto de verano*, *horchata*, *granizado de limón*, *café con hielo* and many others. Find out more in the A–Z of Wine and Drink section.

Wine-Producing Regions

Spain has a 1,000-year-long tradition of wine production. It became firmly rooted during medieval times when, as the Christian kingdoms of the north began to reconquer the land abandoned during the period of Arab occupation, they started to replant the vineyards.

In this regard, the oldest wine-producing areas are Ribera del Duero, Rioja and Penedès. The southern 'Jerez' wines were the first to be exported, becoming popular in England from the 15th century onwards. After a decline in production, wine production in the mid-19th century began to follow the new Bordeaux system for ageing wine in wooden casks.

Spanish wine experienced a golden age from the 1860s onwards, particularly after France was hit by the phylloxera louse, but plague and the Spanish Civil War in the 1930s provoked crises that affected 'quality wine' consumption and export, resulting in a massive loss of vineyards.

The wine industry that developed thereafter, in the 1960s and 1970s focused on common table wine or *vino de mesa*, young, cheaper concoctions for everyday use. The present-day producers of fine wine, based on Bordeaux systems, expanded in the 1980s and 1990s, encouraged by successful exports as well as the vibrant Spanish wine culture.

Spanish wine is subject to regional regulations designed to ensure production quality. Quality wines (*vinos de calidad*) are organised in *Denominaciones de Origen* (*DO*), a regional quality control system similar to the French *appellation contrôlée*. There are around 65 DOs in Spain; the most prestigious are Rioja, Ribera del Duero, Penedès, Priorat and Jerez. Table wines (*vinos de mesa*) are more modest. Within these, better examples carry the label 'wine of the land' (*vino de la tierra*) linking them to a region, such as Vino de la Tierra de Cádiz, like French *vins de pays*. Generally cheap and reasonably good, they include some real bargains.

Other elements that determine the wine's quality are the ageing process, the grape variety and the year of harvest. Young wines show the harvest year, e.g. *Cosecha 2006*. Mature wines in oak casks show ageing categories: *Crianza, Reserva, Gran Reserva*; for example, *Reserva 1999*.

(In the following pages, the denominated areas (DOs) are given in bold.)

RIOJA

Rioja is the name of a region in Northern Spain and of the DO wine-producing area that lies within it along the Ebro valley. It also comprises several counties in the Navarra and Alava provinces. This is the most prestigious DO of Spain, with around 500 firms producing more than 1,500 wines. Rioja is famous for mastering blending and ageing techniques, and some firms do not own vineyards at all, so what you are buying is their blending skill and brand name.

The characteristic that distinguishes Riojas as Spanish wines is a distinct flavour of vanilla, which comes from storage in oak casks. They have a softer, less delicate, but fruitier taste than French wines of equal quality. Rioja also makes respectable white wines.

On the one hand, there are the traditional houses that believe in maturing the wine in oak casks (see *crianza*) until it absorbs a positive flavour of oak. Marqués de Murrieta is the most imposing of these, but others are Paternina, Montecillo, CUNE and Bodegas Riojanas. Some newer firms, such as Muga, make quality wines the old way, too. The easiest to remember are the 'three mighty Ms'– Muga and the Marquéses of Murrieta and Riscal. The law specifies minimum periods in the barrel, but traditional houses may exceed this, and older wines are also likely to have a longer barrel age – La Rioja Alta's Viña Ardanza, for example.

On the other hand, there are the modern *bodegas* that have gone for the minimum barrel ageing. They favour maturing in the bottle instead. Marqués de Cáceres and Langunilla are in this camp, along with Olarro and Spain's third biggest exporter, Faustino Martínez (the labels have a face on them). The last two are popular in the US. Other mid-range popular reds are Berceo, Berberana, LAN and Campo Viejo.

Almost all white Rioja wine is made from the traditional Viura grape. White wine is also made in two different styles. The traditional way is to age it in oak, like red wine. Marqués de Murrieta is the most renowned white in this style. Try their *reserva*, which is lemony, but rich and buttery with the flavour of oak, or Monte Reál from Bodegas Riojanas or a white from López de Heredia. Another popular white is CUNE's Monopole blanco. This has only a modest amount of oakiness, and a freshness that is halfway to the second, newer style – these are more like French wines and are made in vats. The results are crisper and fresher, with more fruit flavour. The best of these is Marqués de Cáceres.

Geography is another important factor in taste. Wines from the Rioja Baja (the lower southern end) are fruitier, everyday wines. The cooler, higher end, the Rioja Alta, produces wines with the highest acidity. This means they are hard when young, but mature into something more complex. Rioja Alta *reservas* are likely to be smooth, firm and high-quality.

There is a third Rioja district, the Rioja Alavesa. The wines are softer, more aromatic and sometimes fuller-bodied.

NAVARRA AND ARAGÓN

Navarra is the district adjoining Rioja, and its wines share many character-istics with those of Rioja. Well-balanced reds are made in the Ribera Alta and lighter versions in Valdizarbe. Excellent reds are made by Asensio, Sindoa and Palacio de Otazu. Young Navarra reds are rather like Beaujolais nouveau. Chivite is the name to look for. Navarra also makes renowned *rosados*: try Gran Feudo.

In Aragón, hefty purplish-coloured reds, often with 15 per cent or more alcohol, are made in Cariñena; they have slightly more balancing acidity than the dull reds from the south. Borja reds are similar, with strong *rosados*, but in Somontano the reds are lighter: try Enate.

NORTHEAST COAST

The main difference between Penedès and Rioja is that Rioja is famed for wine aged in oak, but Penedès chose the French style of reducing time in the cask and bottle ageing instead – and introduced French grapes. This gives the red wines a fruitier taste. Penedès is predominantly a white wine region, however, with good vines growing in the cooler hills. It is one of the main areas of experiment in Spain, the best wines being made from acclimatised foreign grapes, or from these mixed with Spanish grapes.

The big producer here is Torres. Their easy summer white wine Viña Sol – fresh, dry and a bit lemony – is made exclusively from Parellada, the Spanish grape, though in the French style. Torres Gran Viña Sol has a slight pineapple taste because half of the grapes used are Chardonnay, while the rich white and much grander Gran Viña Sol 'Green Label', made with some Sauvignon grapes, is unusual both in being estate-bottled (at Castell de Fransola) and as one of the few white wines matured in oak.

Mas Comtal produces the best rosés, and René Barbier makes intense, more accessible wines.

The heavy wheel of a traditional fruit press.

Far less red wine is made. Gran Sangre de Toro, deep red and fruity, is one of the few still typical of wines from times past. Nowadays, Cavas Avinyó and Cavas Ferret are producing very elegant red wines.

Firms such as Masia Bach specialise in old indigenous vines. This company makes one of the few fresh, sweet Spanish whites (see Dessert Wines, page 102).

Another experimental (and tiny) firm is owned by the American Jean León, who specialises in classic imported vine varieties. Raimat, in the Costers de Segre, is known for quality wines, one being a Cabernet Sauvignon; Raimat Abadia includes this grape. Raimat also makes a rich buttery-tasting white from another grape new to Spain, Chardonnay. Comalats is producing consistent reds, and Castell del Remei has both brilliant whites and reds. Conca de Barberá is another emergent DO. Big Penedès and Cava firms, such as Torres and Codorníu, produce whites that follow modern Catalan methods. Excellent whites are also produced by Concavins.

Alella is a DO whose whites are popular in Barcelona, for the district is just north of the city. Marqués de Alella makes delicate young white wines, with a prickly edge, and Alta Alella produces intense and well-balanced reds. Tarragona is also white wine country, and famed for dessert wines – and for making communion wines.

An important new Catalan DO is Terra Alta, in Tarragona. It is producing outstanding reds, such as Pinol's L'avi Arrufi, or Clúas' Mil.lenium 2001.

The best red – powerful, classic and full-bodied – comes from Priorato. Famous for its quality reds, it is now focused on its mid-range offerings. Alvaro Palacios produces exceptional wines at high prices; and de Muller sells accessible but delicious reds. Look for labels with angels on ladders or 'Scala Dei'. Ampurdán makes good *rosados* and the light red *vi novell*.

Newly planted vines in Spain's largest wine region – Valdepeñas.

LA MANCHA AND VALDEPEÑAS

La Mancha is a vast area containing half of Spain's vineyards. The wine is rough – deep yellow not white – made from the Airén grape. Although La Mancha is still too big to be consistent, more and more quality wines are produced each year. Valdepeñas is a small wine area in the south almost enclosed by the larger La Mancha district and making better-quality wine. Traditionally, Valdepeñas is famous for *aloques*: strong but light reds, made from a blend of red and white grapes. Now the better reds are made with fruity Cencibel, and there are some oak-aged wines at Señorío de Los Llanos. Near Toledo, Marqués de Griñón makes fine Cabernet Sauvignon.

LEVANTE AND THE SOUTHEAST

The hot plains and hills of the southeast are Spain's largest producers of red wine: high-alcohol reds, with no acidity, which makes them taste very dull. Alicante reds are typical, though Utiel-Requena makes a lighter and more acid red and the area's best, most fragrant light *rosado*. Jumilla produces dark, full-bodied and lethal reds, with an alcohol content of up to 18 per cent. Red Yecla is bigger-bodied, though a bit lower in alcohol. Valencia is Spain's chief wine port, and its local wine is white, the best being from Alto Turia. However, for a refreshing, fruity local wine anywhere in southeast Spain, a good bet might be *rosado*.

THE SOUTHWEST

Many Spanish white wines taste remarkably like sherry, though in Spain sherry is often the wine drunk with fish anyway. The white wines of Extremadura, through the DO Ribera del Guadiana, fall into this category. Also, Vinos de la Tierra de Cadiz produces white wines out of the Jerez DO area; among them, try Barbadillo, Cañamero and Vino de Chiclana.

The most famous of these comes from Montilla-Moriles – Amontillado is derived from the name. One of the best-known Finos in the south is Alvear's CB – not in fact a sherry. The Condado de Huelva is known for its sherry and *generoso,* but it increasingly makes white table wines as well.

THE NORTHWEST AND CENTRAL NORTH

The cooler, wetter north is celebrated for fresh white wines, made in traditional ways from traditional Spanish grapes. In the Basque country the *txacoli* white tastes of apples, is rather acid, and slightly *pétillant.*

In Galicia, there is also a small class of 'green' wines. Made in Ribeiro and the Rías Baixas, these taste quite Germanic. Here the Albariño grape makes delicately fruity wines, which prickle slightly in the mouth. The red wine most drunk in Galicia is the fruity, light-coloured El Bierzo.

CASTILLA LEON

In Old Castile, León makes some good oak-aged reds, especially from the Palacio de Arganza, Look for the acronym VILE – they aren't, but avoid the black wines of Orense, which are. Cigales makes *clarete* by mixing black and white grapes. Toro, reputedly the oldest red wine in Spain, is the newest *Denominación de Origen.* Full-bodied with a hint of damson, it has a pleasantly lingering aftertaste. Bodegas Fariña is the name to look for.

In the north of Old Castile, Rueda has had a boom in pleasant, fruity, young whites, which are not very alcoholic, made from the Verdejo grape.

Both Marqués de Griñón and Marqués de Riscal (which make red wines elsewhere – Riscal in Rioja) make excellent white wines here.

Ribera del Duero produces what is indisputably the most famous red wine in Spain: Vega Sicilia. Younger, but still expensive, Valbuena comes from the same place. This is one of the most important red wine-producing regions in Spain. Sure bets include Protos, Pingus (expensive) and Arzuaga. The local Ribera del Duero co-operative makes the affordable fruity Peñafiel. To the east, Burgos makes a light *clarete.*

A Selection of Wines

Spain also produces a range of fortified, dessert and sparkling wines, using local and imported methods. Here's a quick look at some of the most important types.

Sherry

Surely among the world's great wines, what is known to us as sherry is really a range of wines produced in the DO Jerez, one of the few areas in Spain with a centuries-long export tradition about which to boast. It is mainly made from the Palomino grape and blended on a *solera* system of stacked barrels in huge buildings likened to 'sherry cathedrals'.

It is a fortified wine (*vino generoso* is the technical name in Spain for *Jerez*), and its high alcohol content has made it a before- or after-dinner wine, though in Spain Fino is drunk as white wine. It is traditional in Spain to have a glass of *copa*, a glass of sherry, when eating tapas. Sherries are ranked for export by sweetness, though in Spain each category can vary quite widely. Fino and Manzanilla are dry, Amontillado is nutty and medium-dry, Palo Cortado comes in sweetness between this and Oloroso, which is a mature, and usually sweeter, sherry.

Dessert Wines

Do not skip this part of the meal, even if you think you don't like sweet wine, for these are the true desserts of Spain.

Masia Bach's Extrésimo *blanco semi dulce* is rare in being both fresh-tasting yet honeyed, because most of Spain's other dessert wines are darker and much stronger.

Muscat is the main grape used to make dessert wines, often left to wrinkle and concentrate on the vine. In Alicante, the Roman Moscatel is one of the finest, while Moscatel de Valencia has a slight orange edge.

More recently, the Pedro Ximénez grape is being used to make dessert wines, incorporating similar drying methods, in Montilla-Moriles, Málaga and Jerez, achieving outstanding results.

In the 18th century, Málaga *Dulce* was famous in Britain as 'Mountain Wine', and again in the 19th century in the US. Drinking it is like sipping sultanas. It certainly makes a much nicer end to a meal than a bad ice-cream. Smooth *lágrima* is the sweetest, while Málaga Virgin is the best known. Or try Scholtz Hermanos Solera 1885, which has a lovely walnut scent.

Vi rancios are made in Alicante and Tarragona using a *solera* system, for they are fortified dessert wines. Tarragona also makes *clásicos*, sweet wines, both red and white, and with over a fifth alcohol!

Cavas

Cavas are light sparkling wines, made by the champagne method in the Cava DO in Catalonia, although the grapes may come from other DO Cava areas. They mainly originate from San Sadurní d'Anoia, where the big houses are based, including Codorníu, the largest champagne-style wine-maker in the world.

Freixenet Cordón Negro (which comes in a distinctive black bottle) is also popular. Some Spaniards like their Cavas on the sweet side. If you do not, look for the word *brut* or *brut natur*; these wines make a great aperitif. There are also lovely, but expensive, *champáns* made from Chardonnay grapes. The best is from Codorníu, but a good alternative comes from Raimat in DO Costers del Segre.

Young Wines

At home, Spaniards prefer to drink uncomplicated *vino corriente*. This is table wine, sold the first or second year after harvesting. These young reds are free of tannin, so they taste fresh and fruity. As a result, they make remarkably pleasant – and pleasantly cheap – drinking. Even in Rioja, Spain's most famous wine area, only 40 per cent of the wine is aged in barrels.

The biggest *bodega* in Rioja is Campo Viejo, and their best seller in Spain is San Ascensio *2° año sin crianza* wine, which means 'sold in the second year after harvest, without wood ageing'. Another household brand of young red Rioja – Ernest Hemingway's favourite – is *Banda Azul 3° año*, from Frederick Paternina, the country's largest exporter. The *3° año* from CUNE, another major firm, is also popular.

Barrels of wine stacked up in Rioja.

A–Z of Spanish Wine and Drink

A

Abocado
Semi-sweet table wine.

Agua helada
Iced water.

Agua mineral
Mineral water. It is sold every-where, sparkling, *con gas*, or flat, *sin gas*. Some is bottled at famous spas such as Lanjarón.

Agua potable
Drinking water.

Aguardiente
Any distilled liquor. The clear, *anís*-flavoured version is a favourite. *Aguardiente de orujo* is a rough grape brandy, like *marc*.

Aguja
Slightly sparkling.

Albariño
The famous 'green' wine of Galicia, flowery but somewhat acid, and good with shellfish. It is made close to the Portuguese *vinho verde* region and comes from the same grape. It also has a slight fizz, though the famous Palacio de Fefiñanes is still. You will find it less sweet than *vinho verde*.

Aloque
Red wine made from white grapes mixed with only 10% red grapes.

These are light but surprisingly alcoholic wines.

Amontillado
A famous style of sherry, amber-coloured, walnut-flavoured and medium-dry, though in Spain there are drier versions too. They are made from Fino, adding more wine spirit to achieve 17% alcohol content and maturing to become softer and darker. The best are old Finos not for drinking young.

Añejo
Old, mature or aged.

Anís
One of Spain's favourite liqueurs, colourless, flavoured with aniseed and made all over the country. Much used for flavouring biscuits and desserts. There are dry (*seco*) and sweet (*dulce*) versions.

Año
Means 'year'; many popular wines are sold the second or third year after harvest.

B

Bebidas
A general word for drinks.

Blanco, vino
White wines. In Spain these come in more varieties than they do in

Rosé and white wines often make for easier, and lighter, drinking in the Spanish sun.

France. Many taste like sherry, particularly from the hot southwest and west. Then there are the aristocratic traditional white versions, aged in oak barrels. French-style whites are made too – crisper, fresh and fruity. There are very few sweet white wines, but more sparkling wines, called Cavas, and many golden dessert wines, from grapes such as Muscat or Malvasía.

Blanco y negro

Iced milk or cream-flavoured ice-cream and coffee, scented with cinnamon.

Bodega

A wine store where wine and sherry are made, and so the company that makes the wine. Brands are very important in Spanish wine.

Botijo

A traditional clay pot with a small opening from which to pour the water contained within; an ancient and miraculous system, from which the water is always cool!

Brut, brut natur

Extra-dry wine. This appears only on sparkling wine.

C

Café

Coffee. Brewed dark and strong in Spain. *Café solo* is black coffee in tiny cups, while *un corto* or *café cortado* is the identical amount of coffee served in a small tumbler with a little milk. *Café con leche* will be half-milk to bring it to breakfast strength. If you prefer it milder, you can ask for '*leche manchada*', which is mainly milk with less coffee, or '*café americano*' ('*solo*' for unmilked, or '*con leche*' with milk), American-style, and it will be diluted with more water. *Descafeinado*, decaffeinated, or *demáquina*, is made in the coffee-machine, and '*de sobre*' is made from little packets of instant. However, if you order iced coffee (*café con hielo*) do not be surprised if a cup of coffee arrives with a glass of ice cubes. Pour the coffee on the cubes – it cools instantly. But if you like sugar, mix it in before, while it's hot. For an Italian-style *ristretto*, ask for '*café italiano*' or '*café sólo corto*'.

Café en grano

Coffee beans (ready-ground).

Calimocho, Kalimotxo

A very popular drink among young-sters, just cheap wine and coke. Similar to *sangría*.

Caña

The national tap beer glass. Between 100 and 200ml (roughly 4 to 7fl oz).

Carajillo, el

A small black coffee with a shot of brandy or *anís* in it. A Catalan joke – the name means a 'willy'. You can also order *carajillo cortado*, and it will come with a squirt of milk.

Castillo, castell

Château-bottled wines. There are comparatively few of these wines in Spain, which means that all the grapes come from the estate. Good examples come from Marqués de Murrieta at Castel Ygay in Rioja,

Churros *and hot chocolate are a famously good combination.*

Torres Gran Viña Sol 'Green Label' at Castell de Fransola and Raimat in Penedès. The best carry the title *vino de pago*, indicating that the wine comes from a single vineyard.

Cavas

Spanish sparkling wines, made by the champagne method, when they acquire their sparkle in the bottle. Well worth trying if you avoid the sweet ones! Codorníu is the world's largest producer.

Cepa

Grape from a single vine.

Cerveza

Spanish lager. As it is good with plenty of flavour, it is not worth paying for *cerveza extranerja* (imported beer). Mahou is the best bitter, and it is also less gassy; it is popular in central Spain. In Catalonia, the main brand is Estella, while in the south, the slightly lighter Cruzcampo is a regional pride and is served extremely cold, on almost every tap. Also try San Miguel or Aguila brands.

Chacolí

See *Txacoli*.

Champán

In popular usage, champagne-style wine, although the term Cava is increasingly used. Champán Francés is French champagne.

Chocolate caliente

Hot chocolate. Try it for breakfast, with crusty rolls to dip into it. The powder or tablets are sold with a thickener already added, and just need hot milk if you wish. In Spain it is usually drunk plain.

Clara

Spanish shandy – a *caña* with *casera*. *Clara con limon* is mixed with lemon soda.

Clarete

A kind of *rosado* wine, but made following the methods for *tinto* (red) wine. It used to be made a lot in Valdepeñas and La Mancha, but its production is decreasing. In rural areas, *clarete* may be used to refer to regular rosé. They have no connection with French claret.

Coñac

Brandy. An extremely popular after-dinner drink – policemen on early-morning patrol and construction workers have a shot with their breakfast coffee for its warming effects. The most popular brands range from higher-quality Independencia, Cardenal Mendoza (very perfumed) and Carlos I; the representative mid-range examples are Magno and Torres; Cheaper versions include Veterano and Carlos III, which are often drunk in *carajillo* coffee.

Copa

Colloquial generic name for a long drink.

Copa de champán

A champagne glass.

Copa de vino
Wine glass.

Copitas
The tall, tulip-shaped glasses from which sherry is drunk. They narrow towards the top to hold the aroma.

Corriente, vino
Also called *vino de mesa* or *vino de la casa*, a table wine sold the year of, or two years after, harvest. Most Spaniards drink this with their meals.

Cosecha
The year of harvest, given on the bottle. Most Spanish wine is drunk young, but the ageing of wine is regulated in three classes, with a minimum number of years for each class. A wine that is old for its class may be a good one, but red wine *sin crianza*, that is, over three years, is a stale bottle.

Cremas
Sweet milky liqueurs. Ask '*¿Es un licor?*' if in doubt. Coffee and chocolate liqueurs (*crema de café y crema de cacao*) are most common, better known with brand names, such as a Bailey's.

Cremat
A potent Costa Brava coffee with brandy and rum, first flamed.

Crianza
'Aged in wood'. It is this that gives Spanish wines their distinctive Spanish taste. The barrels are made of oak, and new barrels make wine taste strongly of vanilla, so this is used, like spices in cooking, to flavour the wine. The labelling laws specify how much time in the barrel each wine must spend in each of the three categories: *crianza*, *reserva* and *gran reserva*. *Crianza* wines must have a minimum ageing time of 24 months, with at least six months spent in the barrel, and the rest of the time in bottles. Some companies decide to exceed the minimums, as part of the house style, which is why some old-fashioned Riojas have a strong whiff of vanilla.

Cubalibre
Rum and coke. Meaning 'Free Cuba', this term is now a bit old-fashioned.

Cubata
A colloquial derivation of the term *cubalibre*, which is much more used nowadays. The word can be used to name other coke and spirit mixes if specified: for example, *cubata de ginebra* (gin and coke), *cubata de whisky* (whisky and coke).

D

DO, Denominación de Origen
Similar to French *appellation contrôlée*, a designated quality control area.

DOCa
Denominacion de Origen Calificada.

Rows of bottles as far as the eye can see, kept cool in the Codorníu cellars.

Indicating a higher-status quality control area, a title that is reserved for Rioja and Priorat wines.

Dulce
Sweet.

E

Embotellado por
Bottled by.

Espumoso
Any sparkling wine.

F

Fino
The most popular of the sherry styles, being dry, light and, at around 15%, the least alcoholic type. It is a blended wine, made in a *solera* system. A small dose of alcoholic spirit is added to the young wine, which still allows a thick yeast, called *flor*, to develop on top. This prevents the wine from becoming oxidised by the air above it. Finos are among Spain's finest white wines.

G

Gaseosa
Fizzy drink. The most popular version is La Casera.

Generoso, un vino
A fortified wine, drunk before or after a meal. Look for DO Jerez, or Condado Viejo de Huelva. These are also made in Rueda and the Ampurdán.

Ginebra

Gin, made by the huge firm of Larios. It is often drunk short with ice and sweet mixers and with soda and lemon, *en pallofa*, as it is called in Menorca. The famous Menorcan gin is Xoriguer.

Granizado de Limón

Iced lemon juice, a popular drink in summer.

Gran reserva

Much of Spain's best wine falls into this category and they are not expensive compared with matured French wines. In exceptional years, the wine-makers will earmark the vintage for preferential treatment. A *Gran reserva* may not be sold until the sixth year after harvest, and a red wine must spend a minimum of two years ageing in oak casks. White and rosé wines must spend at least six months in the casks and a total of four years (the rest in bottles) before sale.

Granvas

A sparkling wine made in tanks and so less good than a Cava.

H

Hielo, con

With ice or 'on the rocks'.

Holandas

Not gin, but grape spirit, distilled in the poorer parts of Spain and used to make sherry and brandy.

Horchata

A creamy drink, sometimes iced, made from ground tiger nuts (see

The perfect antidote to the hot Spanish midday sun is a glass of freshly pulped fruit juice.

chufa in A–Z of Foods), sweetened with honey. It is sold freshly made in Levante and Madrid.

I

Infusiones

Herbal teas (also called *tisanas*) are very popular in Spain. Camomile is *manzanilla* (don't get it confused with the sherry of that name), either bitter or sweet. Mint tea is *poleomenta*, *tila* is lime and *hierba luisa* is lemon verbana.

J

Jerez

Sherry is the English mispronunciation of the region of Jerez. In Spain, it refers to a range of fortified wines, or *generosos*, produced in this region. These are Fino, Manzanilla, Amontillado, Palo Cortado and Oloroso. It is a fortified wine drunk as an aperitif outside Spain. But Spaniards think of Fino as a dry white wine. It should be drunk from a half-bottle, poured into it directly from the barrel, and kept on ice.

Jugo de fruta

Fruit juice. *Pomelo*, *limón* and *naranja* are grapefruit, lemon and orange. *Manzana* and *piña* are apple and pineapple; *melocotón y uva* is peach and grape.

L

Lágrima, vino de

Wine from 'tears', is juice from grapes that are so ripe that it drips without crushing. As a result the wines are dark gold, with a luscious sweet finish.

Leche

Milk. This is safe but homogenised, in UHT packs, so not particularly attractive to drink. Several big firms also sells pasteurised milk in plastic or glass bottles, which makes a better cup of British tea. Flavoured milk is a *batido*.

Leche merengada

A summer drink, and sometimes an ice, of milk with sweet meringue.

Licor

Liqueur. These take the place of desserts to make a sweet finish to the meal. Two popular examples are the Catalan Calisay, a quinine-based, herbal liqueur with a sweetish aftertaste – good 'on the rocks'. Licor 43 (Cuarenta y tres) is clear orange in colour, vanilla-flavoured and sweet, with a lingering finish. Other common choices are Licor de Hierbas (herbs), Licor de Manzana (apple) and Licor de Melocotón (peach). See *pacharán*.

Limonada

Sweet fizzy lemonade. Popular brands are Fanta, in one-person cans, and La Casera, a slightly lemony-tasting soda, used for diluting drinks. In Madrid's San Isidro festivals it refers to a kind of white wine or vermouth *sangría*, with lemon or natural lemon juice with sugar and water.

M

Malvasía
A sweet dessert wine that takes its name from the grape that also makes Malmsey.

Manzanilla
The driest and most delicate of the pale-gold sherries. The taste comes from the practice of storing chosen light Fino sherries at Sanlúcar de Barrameda by the sea, where they pick up that faint salty tang. It has taken the name of camomile.

Manzanilla
Camomile. A popular herbal tea.

Mini
A 1-litre cup often used in bars or in street festivals for group drinking. Most commonly served in it are tap beer, *sangría*, *mojito*, *calimocho* or any soda and spirit drink.

Mistela
Grape juice mixed with wine alcohol: an aperitif.

Mojito
Rum, sugar, lemonade and mint leaves. A Cuban cocktail, very popular in Spain.

Moscatel
The Muscat grape gives its name to many sweet wines. In the south and Valencia, they are famous for their sultana taste, though the old versions often taste like toffee too. The best come from Málaga, though they are also made in Asturias and Penedès.

O

Oloroso
Dark golden, this is the most full-bodied type of sherry. It is usually sweet and at least 18% alcohol. All sherry starts off dry and develops in contact with the air – unlike wine. Olorosos are developed in a different *solera* from Finos. The new wine is fortified with more spirit at the beginning, and no yeast will grow on this. Olorosos mature by gradually oxidising, and the good ones are reminiscent of port, though there are drier versions. 'Cream' sherry is made by adding juice from Pedro Ximénez grapes.

P

Pacharán or Patxarán
The top generic liqueur in Spain. Made from sloes, red or brown, sweet and *anís*-flavoured, it is worth trying 'on the rocks' before or after meals. Zoco is the best known.

Palo cortado

A rarer type of sherry because it occurs by accident. It is darker than Amontillado and in terms of sweetness comes between it and Oloroso.

Pedro Ximénez

One of the sherry grapes, all of which start dry. But is also used for luscious dessert wines produced in the Montilla-Moriles DO area, and its juice is added to *oloroso*, to make a 'cream' sherry.

Pomada

A popular Menorcan drink, drunk at summer festivals. It is a mix of Xoriguer gin from Mahon with lemon soda (such as Fanta or Kas). The name refers to its soft taste, in contrast to the ease with which it goes to your head!

Ponche

This herbalised old brandy comes in a silver bottle: it is sweeter than ordinary brandy but less sticky than a liqueur. De Soto has a faint taste of orange. *Ponche* means 'punch' and includes drinks such as hot milk whisked with brandy and egg yolks.

Porrón

A wine bottle with a long spout for communal drinking without touching the mouthpiece.

Punys d'ous

A milk punch from Menorca, which also contains rum, lemons, eggs and sugar.

Q

Queimada

A powerful drink said to need three men – two to hold up the man who drinks it! Making it is a magic ritual in Galicia, where *aguardiente de orujo* is poured into a bowl with sugar and apple slices or coffee beans and then flamed. Drinking starts when the flames die down. In ancient times, it was said to be a ritual drink prepared for *meigas*, the local Celtic witches.

R

Rancio, vi (vino)

This mellowed dessert wine is fortified then aged in contact with the air, either in glass jars, left in the sun, or in a *solera* of oak casks. The 20-year-old Fondillón is famous.

Rebujito

A popular Andalucían drink consisting of Manzanilla mixed with *casera* or some other kind of *gaseosa*, such as 7 Up. It is consumed a lot at Andalucían festivals. The name refers to its explosive fizziness.

Refrescos

'Cool' drinks, implying soft drinks.

Reserva

These are the wines you are most likely to find back home – of reasonable quality, with some ageing. They are wines not sold after harvest. Whites and *rosados* have spent at least six months in oak casks plus 18 months in bottle (so a minimum two years in total), and reds at least a year plus 30 months in bottle (so a minimum of three years before sale), often much more. The result is a well-balanced wine, with a satisfying aftertaste. *Reservas* include both modest wines labelled only with the region, and branded wines from companies in good areas such as Rioja and Penedès.

Ribeiro

A white wine produced in Rías Baixas, on southern Galicia's coast.

Ron

Rum. Spain grows sugar cane and makes rum, dark rum and the famous colourless Bacardi (under licence), which is drunk simply with lemon juice and ice or as a *cubalibre*, with coke.

Rosado

Rosé wine. Those from Navarra are well finished and *rosados* are also made in Aragón and Ribera del Duero. On the southeast coast, where the red wine is soupy and very alcoholic, they make a good buy. Try the version made in Tarragona or the cherry-coloured *rosado* from Ampurdán. Utiel-Requena produces a pale, refreshing *rosado*.

S

Sangría

The celebrated chilled wine punch dilutes the southern red wine, which is very high in alcohol, with citrus juice, ice and cold water – and adds a kick again with brandy. Nowadays it is often made with sweet fizzy mixers (See recipe, page 146).

Seco

Dry.

Sidra

Cider. Typical in Asturias, where it is produced and consumed in *siderías*. Also popular in the Basque Country. It is poured over the head with one arm stretched up, into the glass in the other hand, which is at waist height; this liberates the fermented gas. This action is called *escauciar la sidra*.

Sifón

Soda water.

Sol y sombra

'Sun and shade' is a hefty drink of sweet dark brandy, with the addition of a slug of *anís*.

Solera

The system in which sherries are blended. The name refers to a stack of barrels, often five rows high. New wine is first sorted by style – either a Fino or Oloroso type. It is then put into the topmost barrel of a *solera* of the same group.

More refreshing and lower in alcohol than wine, sangría can be bought ready-made.

As wine is taken from the older barrels, so they are each topped up from barrels of younger wine. Fino wine for sampling is drawn from the bottom row, using a little cup on a long stem, called a *venencia*, and then thrown in a great arc into a glass. The best and most expensive sherries come direct from the *solera*, that is, without any further blending.

T

Té con leche
Tea with milk. *Con limón* comes with lemon, while iced tea is *té helado*.

Tinto, vino
Red wine. Usually a better bet in Spain.

Txacoli, chacolí
The Basques are proud of this thin, rather acidic, white wine from vineyards by the sea. It has a faint taste of apples.

V

Verde, vinho
'Green wines'. These are the fresh whites of Portugal.

Vermú
Vermouth. A dry version with ice is *vermú blanco seco con hielo*, a popular lunchtime drink in Spain. *Vermú dulce* is darker and richer, and is still on tap in many mandrilian *tascas*.

Vi novell
New wine. An Ampurdán wine modelled on Beaujolais nouveau.

Vino
Wine, pronounced with a soft B –
'*bino*'. A *viña* is a vineyard, while
vino de pasas refers to home-made
raisin wine.

Vino de mesa, de pasto
Table wine.

Vino de Oporto
Port.

Vino de pago
Supposedly, the highest step on
the Spanish wine quality ladder,
this refers to a wine produced
completely within a lot or a
vineyard, through all of its stages.
It is thus similar to a French
chateâu wine, and implies a
stricter production area, but
this does not necessarily imply a
higher-quality wine.

Vino de la tierra
A category for the better *vinos
de mesa* that still do not fulfill
the conditions necessary to be
considered for a DO quality control
area. A mid-range quality label,
these wines are often reasonably
cheap and sometimes provide a
real bargain.

Vodka
Just as it looks. With tonic it is
y tónica.

W

Whisky sífon
Pronounced 'wihky', with soda.

Z

Zumo de fruta
Fruit juice; see *jugo de fruta*.

Zumo de naranja natural
Freshly squeezed orange juice.

Zurracapote
A red Rioja punch, sometimes
boiled, with cinnamon and brandy.
Often called *zurra*.

Eating Out

In Spain you can really go to town at lunchtime, and eat a lighter meal in the evening.

When and Where to Eat

Though Spaniards eat a light breakfast, you may want to stoke up with fruit and eggs, because lunch is normally eaten late. If you are going out to lunch, remember that Spaniards expect to eat between 2 and 4pm – and this is the main meal of the Spanish day. Supper is then of the soup and eggs sort, though proper dinners are served at every restaurant.

Olives, the simplest Spanish tapa

There is no shortage of cafés and bars in Spain. In simple *tascas* you will find standing only, but elsewhere you can sit. All offer a choice of hot food.

Both smart *restaurantes* and the more modest *hosterías* (inns) may well offer local dishes (*platos típicos*), and there is surprisingly little difference between the types of dishes in the two places. The state-run tourist hotels, the *paradores*, have a policy of offering local food, often in historical buildings. During festivals and in mid-season these can become very busy, but they normally have room.

A *marisquería* specialises in shellfish, while a *merendero* is a casual outdoor eatery, often serving fish. Popular beaches also have *chiringuitos* serving drinks and some food. *Paella* or other rice dishes are the best choice in Levante (Valencia's coast) and fresh fish and shellfish are spectacular on the Costa del Sol (Andalucía).

The modest roadside *venta* (the same word means 'sale', but here it really means 'inn') usually sells hot food as well as drinks and ices.

For afternoon tea, many *pastelerías* (pastry shops) also have a few tables, while you might find a *salón de té*. *Cafés* specialise in coffee, beer and ice-creams rather than just food.

EATING THROUGH THE DAY

A bar is the place to buy breakfast in Spain, usually a quick affair of coffee and bread, though some specialise in chocolate and *churros*. Early risers may then have a snack mid-morning, for lunch is late, rarely before 2pm and often as late as 4pm. Children have a *merienda*, (snack) when they come home from school, and adults may have a coffee or a beer. *Tapas* (bar snacks) start about 7pm, to fill in time before dinner or supper. This will be a lighter meal, eaten around 9pm at home or in restaurants. The south keeps later hours, 10 or 11pm in town, and later still in Madrid.

EATING TAPAS

Tapas (bar snacks) are served with all drinks. Their origin goes back to the 18th century, when King Charles III issued a law obliging taverns to serve a small dish as a 'lid' (*tapa* means lid) covering every pitcher of wine sold, with the lid carrying some kind of snack. This measure was for public health and to prevent drunkenness in the streets. These used to be free, and marinated olives and salted nuts may still be 'on the house', but you will have to pay for other snacks. In the south there are areas where the tradition still holds, such as in Almería, where you may find a drink will cost 2 or 3€, but you'll get such big servings of tapas that you'll have had a meal after a couple of drinks. This happens too in some rural areas of Spain.

Cheese, raw ham and *chorizo* on bread are basic, as is cold potato *ensaladilla* and fried squid (*calamares*) in the south. Prawns are universal (and expensive) and on the north coast there will be potted crab and clams and mussels in wine. Fried fish is popular in the south – try shark in batter (*cazón en adobe*). All sorts of good things are deep-fried – croquettes and cheesy puffs with vegetables or ham. Then there are varieties of foods in sauce, such as meatballs (*albóndigas*) and tripe (*callos*). Finally, there is chicken in garlic and miniature pork kebabs (*pinchos morunos*). A *pincho de tortilla* is a portion of potato omelette with bread on the side.

In popular bars a selection is laid out under glass. In the Basque Country, *pintxos* means tapa or *canapé*. *Vamos de pinchos* means 'We're going out looking for tapas'– a tapas crawl! For just a tiny sample, ask for *una tapa*. *Una ración* is a more substantial portion, enough for two or three to share – and makes a cheap way of eating out quickly.

At the Restaurant

Restaurant meals are usually leisurely. If you are in any sort of hurry, the set menu will come faster. Cooking methods in Spain tend to be straight-forward, portions are enormous and almost everything is served with bread to mop up the juices – though your plate may end up covered with bones from either meat or fish. There is very little highly spiced food.

Spanish seafood is world-renowned.

In Spain, you should expect the soup or salads, then any egg dishes or vegetables, to be served as separate courses before the main course. Salads are generally put on the table before the main course, rather than after it.

Soup may be based on clear broth from the stockpot (*caldo*) or may be a *potaje*, which is thick with vegetables. A popular soup is made of shellfish (*sopa de mariscos*). *Crema de calabacines, calabaza, zanahorias, espárragos* or *champiñones* (courgette, pumpkin, carrot, asparagus or mushroom soup) are usually creamy home-made soups.

Entremeses de carne is a selection of cold meats, but

ensalada mixta, salad with tomato and tuna, is one of the most popular starters.

Egg dishes such as *tortilla*, which is not an omelette but more like a cake of egg, and *huevos a la flamenca*, eggs in a wonderful mixed vegetable sauce (see recipes, page 130), make a main dish if you are not hungry. *Paella* and pasta dishes are also considered starters if you order an individual portion, but in specialised restaurants (more likely on the coast), if you order a whole *paella* for a party to share it is considered a main course.

Vegetable dishes tend to be massive, while the bean dishes are soupy stews, with plenty of liquid and are a meal in themselves.

Fish cooked *a la plancha* is from the griddle, *a la parrilla* it is grilled (often on charcoal), while *la barbacoa* refers to an outside grill. If you prefer fish with sauce, try *merluza en salsa verde*, or *a la vasca* (see recipe, pages 137–8). Meat, poultry and fish used to be served by themselves, with bread, though many dishes now come with potato chips. Fried and roast chicken (*pollo frito* or *asado*) and pork chops (*chuletas de cerdo*) are universal. But lamb chops (*chuletas de cordero*) are more of a luxury. If the restaurant advertises that its

oven is *un horno* (an old-fashioned bread oven), the roast lamb will be a real treat. *Una caldereta* is a stew.

Spaniards mainly close a meal with fruit; in general, the desserts, pastries and ice-creams are not good. However, the classics such as *crema catalana* and *tocino de cielo* or *tarta de Santiago* can be delicious and are worth trying once. The cheese selections are not large, and soft cheeses may be served with honey or sugar as a dessert. A finishing sweet touch to a meal is more likely to come from a *coñac* (brandy), which is usually sweet and often perfumed, or from herb or fruit liqueurs, such as *pacharán*.

Saffron-infused fish and potatoes – what could be finer?

One of the joys of a trip to Spain is the leisurely outdoor dining.

HAVING A DRINK

Spaniards make an occasion of pre-dinner drinking. Apart from beer and sherry, sweet drinks such as vermouth on ice or the *anís*-flavoured, brandy-like *pacharán* are popular aperitifs. Gin is also served with sweet mixer-syrups. Mineral water or even *gaseosa*, a fizzy lemonade, are used to dilute the table wine.

At the end of the meal, both men and women enjoy sweet liqueurs. When ordering brandy (*coñac*), you will always be asked which type you prefer: some are sweet and perfumed and others resemble French *cognacs*.

PAYING THE BILL

You are unlikely to be hurried through your meal, and the bill will come only when you ask for it. Some places include service on the bill. There is no fixed rate for tipping in restaurants, although generally 5–10% of the bill is appreciated. Some people prefer to leave a pile of whatever small coins they happen to have in their pockets.

SMOKING

You will now find separate non-smoking sections provided in Spanish restaurants and bars that are bigger than 100 square metres. However, in reality you'll find that many eating places are smaller than that, in which case they will be either smoking or non-smoking. And as many people smoke in Spain, most will be of the former variety.

Special Requirements

When arriving at a restaurant, if you have any special dietary requirements be sure to indicate this to the waiters and they will do their best to help.

VEGETARIANS

Spanish food is largely peasant cooking, based on good vegetables. Many restaurants have pictures of dishes outside. However, vegetarians should beware! Many soups, vegetable dishes and *paellas* contain small amounts of bacon or sausage. There is also a tradition of cooking in pork fat. The only way to find out is to ask.

Another thing to beware of is *cuajada*, which looks like yoghurt; it is junket, and so is set with animal rennet (*cuajo*).

Many pastries are, or used to be, made with lard or oil.

GLUTEN-FREE DIET

Bread is the accompaniment to every Spanish meal, as meat, fish and poultry are normally served without vegetables. Ask for a side order of boiled potatoes (*una ración de patatas hervidas*), though it will be easier to get chips (*patatas fritas*). The good news is that there are many dishes that are not flour-based, particularly grills and rice.

Flour is used in wine-based sauces and in batter. Bread is commonly used in soups as a thickener, and is puréed for sauces, particularly those that contain nuts.

Among tapas, avoid the Basque *bola*, which is a *béchamel*-based croquette and all *buñuelos*: many are based on choux pastry. Cocoa is sold mixed with a flour thickener.

MILK-FREE DIET

Milk has a low standing in the Spanish kitchen, being kept for young children. Cream is not much used, either, except in the north. Avoid wine-and-cream sauces,

The markets offer a kaleidoscope of colour.

but the majority of creamy puddings are based on eggs or ground almonds.

CHILDREN

Spanish children eat out in restaurants with their parents from their early years, and so they learn how to behave considerately. Children are welcomed everywhere except, perhaps, in the smartest of restaurants. The portions in Spain are enormous, so most small children eat off their mother's plate.

Finding food for children is not difficult, because the tapas dishes sold in bars are ideal for the young. Most children like *calamares* (squid rings), which look vaguely like onion rings, while dishes such

as meatballs in tomato sauce are universal. Don't be put off by sherry sauces – the cooking process destroys the alcohol. Fried fish is of better quality than elsewhere – with the ever-popular chips. *Hamburguesas* (hamburgers) are not recommended.

For breakfast, try hot chocolate, for Spanish milk is homogenised and not particularly pleasant to drink on its own. Nesquik or ColaCao are good for making cold chocolate drinks, and they are also served with hot milk.

Cafés and bars are open at lunch and before the late supper hours of Spain. Many bars also have a salon or dining room, where you can sit down and order from the menu.

Enjoying a drink in the sunshine of Madrid's busy Plaza San Andreas.

Eating In

Catalan olive oil, infused with a variety of herbs and spices, makes a beautiful display.

Shopping

Supermarkets have come to Spain in a big way, but you will also find many corner stores, specialist food shops and lots of lively street markets.

If you can, find a market or, if you go to a *Hiper* or a *Supermercado* (both vast supermarkets) early in your visit, bulk shopping will save you a lot of money. Equally, don't be embarrassed about buying in very small quantities. Spanish people point and often buy l00g (¼lb) at a time.

Un almacén is a big store, *una tienda de comestibles* a food shop and *una tienda de alimentacíon* is a general grocery. *La panadería* sells only bread and breakfast pastries (doughnuts, *palmeras*, *napolitanas*), but in *una pastelería* you can get sweet breakfast rolls as well as cakes and biscuits. Your children may pester you to stop at *una tienda de chucherías,* a sweet stall.

You will find most of the items you buy at home in Spanish supermarkets – with small differences. For instance, canned tomatoes come in three convenient varieties. *Pelado* are whole tomatoes, while *triturado* are minced and *frito*

Experience a Spanish market if you can.

is a thick tomato sauce, which drowns everything if you use too much. Don't buy *tocino* if you want breakfast bacon because it is solid fat from the pork belly, with no lean meat. It is usually chopped and fried with vegetables. Ask for *beicon* instead. Butter quickly loses its pleasant taste; margarine, sold in tubs, makes a better spread.

MEAT AND POULTRY

As well as the useful 'spit-roast chicken' stalls found in large villages at the weekend, Spain has specialist shops, called *pollerías*, that sell chickens and eggs. Most supermarkets and butchers also sell fresh and frozen chicken.

The Spanish meat shop, the *carnicería*, looked rather medieval until recently, with lumps of meat on hooks. You can also buy meat from supermarkets, where it will be cut to order; normally the raw and cooked meat sections will be next to each other. Spaniards eat quite a lot of mince, in meatballs and stuffed vegetables. Try the less-familiar veal mince, or a mixture made with pork or ham.

The *charcutería* is a cold-cuts shop and, by the way, meat from the bullfight is not sold in ordinary butchers (see *carne de lidia*).

Ternera is a cross between beef and veal, and makes good chops and steaks. However, most families eat pork as their main meal. Small village shops often have a chilled cabinet with chops and a boned loin of pork for slicing. Lamb is a luxury, and chops most of all. Stewing lamb is sold with all the bones in, but is good. In the south, kebab meat is sold cubed and marinated.

Raw ham is used a lot in Spanish recipes. The cheapest type of *serrano* (off the bone) is in the cabinet with the cold meat and a bit will be cut to order for you.

Think of red *chorizo* as a very tasty sausage. There's one for cooking and a cured version for eating raw. It is much more meaty than British sausages. Those with a red string are often very hot (*picante*), while a white string means it is mild. The whitish *butifarra* is made from veal and pork, for grilling, while *longaniza* and black puddings such as *morcilla* are cut up and used to flavour bean dishes.

You will also find a 'deli' section in most large butchers, which stocks cooked and ready-to-eat cured meat.

FISH

Spaniards love fish and eat it about three times a week. Spain has some of the best fish in Europe; it is sold fresh everywhere and there is a considerable choice. In the Cádiz, Huelva and Sevilla areas there are also *freidurías*, take-away fried fish shops.

Spain is very regional: fish are called different names in different places, and one name can be used for several different fish. Fish are sorted by size – this is confusing, until you realise that the same fish appear in different piles. Tiny sardines under 2cm (¾in) long are for deep-frying, and the normal-size fish are for grilling. Larger hake (*merluza*) are for cooking, but the little ones (*pescadillas*) are chopped up to make fish soup, Unsorted (mixed) prawns can be cheaper than sorted ones.

Basically, oily fish such as mackerel are best grilled. If they look like meat steaks, such as swordfish or tuna, they need lots of oil while grilling. Pinkish-fleshed fish, sold skinned, need an acid marinade, or lemon juice and capers to serve. White fish can be cooked every way.

Grilling is easiest, although barbecuing is more fun if you have outside space for a fire. Frying is easy for two, but hard work for more people, because there are rarely enough pans, or space, in a Spanish kitchen.

Many Spanish recipes start with fish in the pan and finish it in the oven with a sauce. A thick fish soup is also a good bet. Shellfish are sold raw and prawns need boiling – three minutes for *gambas* and five or six for *langostinos* and *cigalas*, depending on size. These are good eaten with coarse salt, and big versions can be barbecued. Bigger clams are usually eaten raw, little ones included in soups and sauces.

Small freezer shops are common in villages and these stock open boxes of fish and also different vegetables. Here you can buy quantities as small as l00g (¼1b) to go in something like a *paella*.

They also offer items like battered crab claws, fish in crumbs and little salted cod pies (*tortas de bacalao*). Don't buy *bacalao* (salted cod) unless you can wait a day for it to soak. After that, it can be used like fresh fish. Salted sardines are sold packed in a fan shape in wooden boxes: rinse first. Many classic dishes, such as *bacalao a la purrusalda* (leek and salted cod soup), are also canned.

CHEESE

The national cheeses are mainly hard and Cheddar-like – and something of an acquired taste. Manchego is the famous name and there are many other cheeses like it. An old, ripened cheese (*añejo*) will be very strong, crumbly and hard, a bit like Parmesan. The same cheese is softer and blander when young (*queso tierno*). You may be asked '*¿Queso de vaca o queso de cabra?*', 'Cows' milk cheese or goats?' as Spain is famous for its sheep's (*oveja*) and goats' cheeses. These are mainly hard or semi-hard cheeses too, all cut in slices from a drum shape, and the main difference is that cows' milk cheese is a bit cheaper. Bland international cheeses such as Edam are also widely sold.

Firm Spanish cheeses grate well and the most successful cooked dish is *queso frito* – slices egged and crumbed, then fried. They are popular to start or end a meal. Queso de Burgos is a famous fresh cheese, available everywhere.

Many areas do make soft fresh cheeses, but they are not so easy to find; nor is cottage cheese, *requesón*. Soft *cuajada* (junket) is more widely distributed. See also the A–Z of Spanish Food.

VEGETABLES AND FRUIT

You will find a good choice of vegetables in markets and in the *verdurería,* the greengrocer. The quality is exceptionally good, the colours bright and prices low.

Learn to use the vegetables available. Chard, with leaves like spinach, is worth a try, and whole artichokes, too. Look up how to eat them in the A–Z of Spanish Food if they are not familiar and then try them out. In summer, Spaniards love salads and *gazpacho*.

PICNICS

The salads in Spain are so delicious and varied that shopping for picnics is a positive pleasure.

The *bocadillo* is one of the nicest sandwiches in the world. Made from a crusty roll, it is split and dribbled with olive oil, instead of butter, which goes off quickly in hot weather. Inside, ham (*serrano*) and cheese are a wonderful combination. *Pa amb tomàquet*, Catalan bread with tomato juice pressed in, is also very good.

There are many other picnic ingredients to choose from. Little cans full of seafood, sold for starters, are particularly good with salad, for example. Vegetables in marinade, eaten with a spoon from the can, are also excellent. Two people can easily finish a can. Many cans have ring-pull openers, but some big litre beer bottles require a bottle opener. Mahou won't, but you'll need it with Cruzcampo and Estrella.

COOKED MEAT

You will find cold meat in supermarkets or in a specialist *charcutería*. They sell the familiar salamis and *mortadelas* and Spanish cold meats. The largest *chorizos*, about 5cm (2in) across, are for slicing and eating raw. Many pressed meats are on offer, made from meat half-minced, half in small pieces. *Pudín de cerdo* is rather like corned beef, but is made of pork.

Spaniards eat a lot of ham. The most expensive is raw *serrano*. But cooked ham is sold everywhere, called *jamon York*, while cured 'ham' pieces of shoulder are good and much cheaper. Cheeses are also sold in *charcuterías*.

Recipes

HUEVOS A LA FLAMENCA
BAKED EGGS WITH GYPSY TRIMMINGS

SERVES FOUR

Slices of sausage (chorizo), bits of ham and prawns can all go into this dish – and all together, if you like – for this is a colourful mixture of whatever comes to hand, baked in tomato sauce.

4 tablespoons olive oil
1 large onion, peeled and chopped
2 garlic cloves, skinned and finely
   chopped
2 *chorizo* sausages, sliced
100g/4oz slice raw *serrano* ham, diced
1 large green pepper, destalked, seeded
   and diced
400g/14oz can tomatoes and juice
salt, pepper and paprika
100g/4oz cooked green beans, cut into
   short lengths
4 or 8 eggs

Heat the oven to high for butane gas (180°C, 350°F, gas mark 4 at home) and put in a *cazuela* or four ovenproof baking dishes. Heat the oil in a frying pan and fry the onions slowly until soft, then add the garlic. Fry the sausage and ham in the pan until cooked, then distribute them between the dish(es) in the oven.

Add the diced pepper to the pan and fry for 3–4 minutes. Empty the tomatoes into the pan, breaking them up with a spoon. Season with salt, pepper and a little paprika and cook until the tomato reduces to a sauce. Add the beans and heat through. Spoon the vegetable sauce over the sausage and ham. Break in one or two eggs per person, then just swirl them lightly into the sauce with a fork. Bake in the oven for about 15 minutes until the eggs are just set. Eat with bread and green salad.

Note. At home you can use smoked gammon cut from a knuckle, which is cheap, instead of *serrano*. Chicken livers go well in it, too.

TORTILLA DE CAMARONES

SPANISH SHRIMP OMELETTE

SERVES FOUR

Spanish omelettes are not like the French versions, but are more like cakes – they come in the shape of a sponge layer. They are often cut like cakes, too, into wedges that go into sandwiches, or are spiked with cocktail sticks, as tapas.

A variety of foods can go into tortillas, with cooked potato and fried onion being popular. But shrimps and small prawns almost always end up in fritters or tortillas, as they are too small to peel for a fish dish. Remember, in Spain they are raw, so will need brief cooking. Camarones are a tiny white variety of shrimp, so small that they are eaten whole, without peeling them or removing the head or tail. This is similar to what happens with chanquetes, *the tiny fish that are a delicious speciality from Málaga.*

Tortilla de Camarones is a speciality of Cádiz. It is different from the traditional Spanish egg-based tortillas in that it is actually a deep-fried, flour-based fritter, and does not usually even contain eggs.

250g/9oz of camarones
parsley (better fresh)
200g/7oz wheat flour
200g/7oz chickpea flour (if you can't find it, use all wheat flour)
½ (or 1 small) onion

175ml/6fl oz olive oil
saffron (better than saffron colouring)
1 to 2 glasses of water
a dash of beer (optional)
a bit of salt

First, put both kinds of flour in a bowl (or all wheat flour, if that is what you are using). Add the onion and parsley and mix. Then add water until you obtain a runny dough. Add saffron and a bit of salt (half a teaspoon) followed by the *camarones*, mixing well after every addition. Some versions also call for a dash of beer, so add this if using. Let the mixture settle in the fridge for 1 hour.

Next heat the oil in a frying pan. Take a serving spoon and pour spoonfuls of the dough into it. If it is a big pan, you can fry several *tortillitas* at once. The dough should spread around the base of the pan. However, if the oil is not deep enough to cover the *tortillitas* completely, you may need to flip them over so that they brown on both sides. It's a quick process, so be careful they don't burn!

Remove the fritters and place them on a paper towel to drain. They are now deliciously crisp and ready to eat!

ENTREMESES ESPECIALIDADES
THREE SPECIAL SPANISH STARTERS

Lettuce and tomatoes always make a great side dish in the Spanish heat, though there are many other refreshing options. The following three dishes are classical Spanish starters.

GAZPACHO ANDALUZ
GAZPACHO FROM ANDALUCÍA

SERVES FOUR TO SIX

This refreshing cold soup from Andalucía will quench your thirst and nourish your spirit if you are feeling overwhelmed by southern Spain's sun and high temperatures. Gazpacho *is very popular among locals, as well as being one of Spain's best-known dishes internationally. There are endless versions, but you'll always find garlic in it. It is usually accompanied by bread.*

2 kg/4lb ripe red tomatoes
1 cucumber
2 green peppers
2–3 garlic cloves
200ml/7fl oz virgin olive oil
75ml/2fl oz vinegar
salt to taste

Wash and chop the vegetables, peeling the cucumber first. Some people also peel the tomatoes, which is easier if you heat them first in hot water (don't boil them). Others leave the skin, thinking that it adds flavour. Put all the chopped vegetables in a big bowl, then add oil and vinegar and blend with a mixer. Add salt to taste. You can add water if you feel the soup is too thick.

Place the bowl in the refrigerator and let the soup cool for an hour. If you don't have time to wait, you can chop up some ice cubes and add them.

Gazpacho is usually served in bowls with hunks of bread for dipping as a side dish. Others prefer to drink it from a glass. Chopped cubes of hard-boiled eggs and *serrano* ham can also be added, according to your taste, and this is a good dish to experiment with.

PAN Y TOMATE CON JAMON
TOMATO-BREAD WITH SERRANO HAM

The Catalans call this dish pan tomaca, and they are so fond of it that I have included it here, even though it seems too simple. First, and essentially, buy good crusty bread and cut it into rounds. Then slice a few ripe tomatoes in half, before crushing them onto the bread, so that it becomes soaked with the juices. Sprinkle some salt on top. Next, dribble with a little olive oil – some people rub it with a garlic clove, too. Finally, top it all with thin slices of serrano ham (called pernil in Catalonia), which is a matter of national pride.

ESPINACAS CON GARBANZOS

SPINACH AND CHICKPEAS

SERVES SIX

Chickpeas with spinach is a very much-loved dish in southern Spain. Like many Mediterranean recipes, its modest ingredients are combined to form a healthy and very tasty result. This dish is normally eaten as a first course, but it is also one of the most popular tapas served in Seville with drinks.

2 bunches of fresh spinach (or 250g/9oz of frozen)
½kg/1lb of chickpeas
4 cloves of garlic
2 slices of bread
1 tablespoon of paprika
1 tsp of ground cumin

olive oil
wine vinegar
hot red pepper if desired
salt to taste

First, soak the chickpeas for 24 hours. Jars of soaked chickpeas are also sold in Spanish supermarkets. These will save you time, but the taste won't be quite the same. Rinse the fresh spinach leaves thoroughly to eliminate any dirt. If preferred, you can also use frozen spinach.

Cook the spinach covered with water over a low heat for 10 minutes.

Meanwhile, put the oil in a frying pan and gently fry the peeled and whole cloves of garlic with the slices of bread. Remove the bread once it is lightly toasted and remove the pan from the heat once the garlic is done.

Next, grind up the bread slices with the vinegar, fried garlic, cumin and red pepper.

Once the oil has cooled down, add the paprika and fry it gently. Then add the ground bread mixture and, lastly, the cooked spinach, which you will have previously chopped up. Fry everything over a low flame, together with the tender chickpeas, for about 10 minutes.

Season the dish to taste and serve with some slices of bread fried in a clay casserole.

Tuna and potato salad – see page 134.

Artichokes are a Spanish favourite.

If the potatoes are small, boil them in their skins until cooked. If they are large, peel and cut them into equal-sized chunks and cook, then drain well in a colander. Peel as soon as they are cool enough to handle and chop into a shallow salad bowl. Chop the onion and scatter over the potatoes. Empty the tuna and its oil into the potatoes and break up the fish with a fork. Sprinkle with salt and pepper and turn gently. Add enough mayonnaise to coat the potatoes to your taste, then sprinkle with capers and serve.

ENSALADILLA DE PATATAS Y ATÚN

POTATO SALAD WITH TUNA AND CAPERS

SERVES FOUR

The secret of really good potato salad is to make it then eat it straight away, while the potatoes are still slightly warm. Any potato left over can be used as a tasty addition to a mixed salad. Spaniards invented anchovy-stuffed hard-boiled eggs, and these go well with it.

1kg/2lb new potatoes
¼ mild Spanish onion
2 (100g/4oz) cans tuna in oil
salt and pepper
300ml/½ pint mayonnaise
2 tablespoons drained capers

ALCACHOFAS SALTEADAS CON JAMÓN

SAUTÉED ARTICHOKE BASES WITH HAM

SERVES FOUR

Artichokes are always on sale in the markets, but many people don't know what to do with them, or find them fiddly to eat whole. This is an easy way to eat them fresh. You can also make this popular dish with canned (and in Spain frozen) bases, or cooked green beans or fresh peas. At home a 500g/1lb bag of frozen broad beans is perfect. Buy the cheaper of the serrano hams for cooking, not the best slices, carved from the bone for tapas.

8 globe artichokes
2 tablespoons olive oil
1 onion, peeled and finely chopped

2 garlic cloves, skinned and finely
  chopped
250g/9oz raw *serrano* ham *para cocinar*,
  cubed
salt and pepper
chopped fresh parsley (optional)

To prepare the artichokes, chop off the
stalks (if they are stringy, that means
the artichokes are tough and will need
an extra five minutes' cooking). Trim the
bottom so it is flat, removing the small
leaves. Turn on its side and cut through
the top leaves, leaving a base about
4cm/1½ inches deep. Trim away the side
leaves with a small knife until the white
base shows through. Cook the bases
in boiling salted water for 10 minutes.
Drain upside down and cool briefly.

Flip off any soft leaf stumps with
your thumb, revealing the choke. Use
a spoon and your thumb to remove
and discard the bristly choke, leaving a
smooth saucer-shaped base. The bases
need about five minutes' more cooking,
either in a frying pan (as in this dish), or
in boiling water if you want to use them
for salad.

Heat the oil in a frying pan and
cook the onion until softened, adding
the garlic near the end. Add the
ham, tossing over a high heat for 1–2
minutes. Quarter the artichoke bases,
add them to the pan and fry for about
5 minutes, stirring occasionally, Season
and serve garnished with parsley, if you
are using it.

SOPA DE PESCADO Y MARISCOS CON NARANJAS

FISH SOUP WITH ORANGE

SERVES FOUR

*Many people don't like to see bones on
their plates, so this is a good method of
serving only the fillets, yet also
using up the heads, bones and skins
that you have paid for. It is also fun to
eat and to shop for the ingredients.
Look at the fish as you are buying
them and imagine that about one third
(from the middle of the back) will be
bone-free white flesh, and the rest can
go into making the soup part. Get the
fishmonger to do the chopping for you:
'limpieles, por favor'.*

*Shellfish that look interesting but
fiddly to open can go in and will be
no problem. The stalks (not heads) of
parsley can go in too, and also any of
those recognisable herbs that get
picked on holiday walks because they
smell nice.*

2kg/4lb mixed fish with heads
2 large Spanish onions, peeled and
  chopped
2 bay leaves
small bunch parsley
handful of herbs, even wild lavender
2 tablespoons olive oil
1 green pepper, destalked, seeded and
  chopped
2 large garlic cloves, skinned and finely
  chopped

2 tablespoons flour

200ml/7fl oz dry white wine

salt, pepper and paprika

your choice of: 200g/7oz prawns and/or
little clams, small crabs, etc.

1 large tomato, skinned and seeded,
flesh chopped

½ dried chilli (*guindilla*) or a little
cayenne

8 small new potatoes (optional)

1 orange

Identify the best bits of the fish and
cut these out quickly, if this hasn't
already been done. There is no need to
be fussy about this, as all the rest will
be used up. Keep the flesh aside on
a plate.

Next put the heads, bones, skin,
etc. in a large saucepan or flameproof
casserole with one chopped onion and
the bay leaves. Cut off and scrunch up
the parsley stalks and add them and
any other herbs. Cover with 1.2 litres/
2 pints water and bring to the boil.
Simmer for 40 minutes, then strain off
the stock.

Heat the oil in a pan, large enough to
take everything and fry the remaining
onion slowly until soft. Add the chopped
pepper, then the garlic.

Sprinkle with flour and cook for
1 minute, stirring, then add the wine.
Season the reserved fish pieces
with the salt, pepper and paprika and
tuck these into the pan, along with
any little crabs, prawns, clams, etc.

Add the chopped tomato flesh, the
chilli and the potatoes (if you are using).
These should be small or cubed to the
size of big marbles. Cut the zest from
the orange in a spiral with a potato
peeler and add.

Squeeze the orange juice. Pour in 1
litre/1¾ pints of fish stock and bring to
simmering point. Cover and cook over
a low heat for 20 minutes, then add the
orange juice. Check the seasoning and
add the parsley.

Note. For a party at home, the stock
can be strained off and 2 tablespoons
of rice cooked in it. This can then be
served first, garnished with chopped
prawns and parsley. You can then serve
the fish with boiled new potatoes as a
main course.

Scampi make a delicious, if messy, treat.

CIGALAS A LA PARRILLA CON ALIOLI

GRILLED SCAMPI WITH GARLIC MAYONNAISE

SERVES FOUR

This is messy to eat, so is a good dish to serve when everyone is in bathing suits. The sauce is very strong – not for anyone who does not like garlic. It is the best accompaniment for grills, and Spaniards serve it with grilled lamb chops and roast lamb.

1kg/2lb raw scampi without heads
a little olive oil
coarse salt
For the *alioli*:
6 garlic cloves, skinned
½ teaspoon salt
2 egg yolks
200ml/7fl oz good olive oil

Make the *alioli* first. Chop the garlic really finely, then sprinkle with the salt. Use the flat side of a table knife to mash it to a paste – or use a pestle and mortar. Put the egg yolks in a bowl and stir in the garlic.

In a Spanish kitchen there is no danger of cold oil, but if you are at home, stand the jug of measured oil in a pan of warm water for a few minutes. Whisk the egg yolks, preferably with an electric whisk, and add a few drops of oil. When these have been incorporated, add a few more – the mayonnaise should thicken quickly. As soon as it thickens, you can start adding the oil faster, beating all the time, until it is incorporated. If you keep the sauce in the refrigerator, place in a screw-top jar or keep well covered.

Light the barbecue and let the fire die down, or heat the grill to high. Brush the scampi with oil and grill for about 8–10 minutes, depending on size. Transfer to a dish and scatter with coarse salt.

The neat way to get scampi out of their shells is to pick one up from the back and press the sides together. This cracks the shell all down the stomach. You can get a thumb under the legs on one side and peel them upwards, to take off a bit of the back shell – like taking off a saddle. After that, pinch the tail fin hard and pull the body. It should pop out when the vacuum is released. To eat, dunk the scampi in the sauce. Plenty of serviettes will be needed.

MERLUZA A LA VASCA

HAKE IN WINE AND SEAFOOD SAUCE

SERVES FOUR

Any white fish can be used for this dish, which children like because the fish doesn't have too many bones, It is finished in the oven, and you can use a big cazuela or one ovenproof dish per person, which is easier. It is good, too, with frozen peas instead of shellfish, but be sure then to include the parsley.

137

4 tablespoons olive oil

250g/9oz onions, peeled and chopped

2 big garlic cloves, skinned and finely chopped

4 tablespoons flour

salt and pepper

1 teaspoon paprika

4 hake steaks or fish fillets, 700g/1½lb

1 medium tomato

300ml/½ pint dry white wine

200ml/7fl oz water with a fish cube, or fish stock

1 bay leaf

250g/9oz baby clams or prawns, peeled

chopped fresh parsley to garnish (optional)

Heat the oven to high for butane gas (180°C, 350°F, gas mark 4 at home). Heat the oil in a frying pan and fry the onions slowly until soft, then add the garlic. Put the flour on a plate and sprinkle with salt, pepper and paprika. Take any loose bones out of the fish, then coat the pieces in the seasoned flour. Push the onion to the sides of the pan and put in the fish, frying it until golden – about 4 minutes on each side. Transfer the fish pieces to an ovenproof dish or dishes and put them in the oven.

Peel the tomato while the fish is frying: ripe skin should strip of easily. Quarter it, then scoop out and discard the seeds. Chop the flesh and add to the pan with a little of the wine. Reduce this, stirring occasionally. Add the remaining wine and water (or stock) and crumbled stock cube if using, plus the bay leaf, and bring back to the boil. Pour over the fish. If individual dishes are being used, you may need a little more liquid. Tuck the clams or prawns round the fish and return to the oven. Reduce the oven temperature (to 160°C, 325°F, gas mark 3 at home) and leave the dish for 10 minutes or so. Serve sprinkled with parsley and eat with crusty bread.

PAELLA VALENCIANA
MIXED RICE WITH CHICKEN
AND SEAFOOD

SERVES FOUR

It's best to eat paella in a restaurant when you are in Spain: they have the pans and space. It is quite hard work to prepare yourself. However, you must have a recipe to take home, to remind you of your holiday. Best to take the rice home, too. This is the easy version, but even so it takes over an hour.

4–5 tablespoons olive oil

l onion, peeled and chopped

2 garlic cloves, skinned and finely chopped

750ml/1¼ pint good stock

200ml/7fl oz dry white wine

30 saffron strands or 2g sachet saffron powder

250g/9oz little squid (or mussels, cleaned)

250g/9oz raw prawns, peeled
salt, pepper and cayenne
4 chicken thighs, or 2 legs, split in half
400g/14oz Spanish medium-grain rice
    (or Italian *risotto* rice)
1 teaspoon paprika
l00g/4oz cooked green beans or peas
200g/7oz canned red pimento, drained
chopped fresh parsley

Use two pans to speed up the frying – a *paella* or wide shallow flameproof casserole big enough to take the complete dish, plus a frying pan. Heat 2 tablespoons of oil in the *paella* pan and fry the onion gently until soft, adding the garlic at the end.

Next, warm the stock and wine, then pour a little of this liquid over the saffron in a cup.

Prepare the shellfish. To clean the squid, first use the tentacles to pull out everything inside, then cut off the heads above the eyes. Discard everything except the tentacles and body. Flex the body to pop out the transparent 'spine'. Wash well, rubbing off the skin, and cut the body into rings.

Heat two more tablespoons of oil in the second pan and put in the squid tentacles and rings. Fry for a couple of minutes, then remove to a plate. Put in the peeled prawns and fry for 2 minutes, then transfer to the plate with the squid.

Rub salt, pepper and cayenne into the chicken pieces. Add more oil to the pan if necessary, then add the chicken pieces and fry for about 10 minutes on each side.

Meanwhile, wash the rice in a sieve and drain. When the onion is ready, add the rice to the *paella* pan and stir it into the onion. Fry for a couple of minutes, stirring, then sprinkle with the paprika. Add the saffron liquid and one-third of the stock and bring to the boil. Timing is essential now, so keep a careful check – cook it for 20 minutes. When the liquid has been absorbed, add another third of the stock and evenly distribute the chicken, squid, prawns and beans or peas round the *paella* pan.

When the liquid has nearly gone, add the remaining liquid and give the mixture a stir. Move the chicken pieces, bedding them into the liquid round the pan. The liquid should all disappear, and cooking time should be up about 6 or 7 minutes later. Test that the rice is cooked.

Cut the pimento into strips and lay these across the rice. Turn off the heat and wrap the *paella* pan in foil then newspaper, to keep in the steam. Let it stand for 10 minutes. The flavours will blend and the last drop of liquid should disappear. Sprinkle with parsley and serve. Spaniards prefer red wine with *paella*.

Note. Packs of small, frozen squid are often sold in larger supermarkets in the UK.

PISTO MANCHEGO CON HUEVOS

VEGETABLE STEW FROM LA MANCHA

SERVES FOUR

A very easy, traditional dish from La Mancha and very popular all over Spain (other regional versions exist). Usually eaten as a first course, it is basically a fresh tomato- and pepper-based vegetable stir-fry, normally accompanied by fried eggs, but it can be served with sausages, bread, potatoes, or even, quite commonly, with cured serrano *ham cubes added to the mixture.*

3 or 4 ripe tomatoes (approx. 500g/1lb)
1 big onion (or 2 small onions)
3 or 4 garlic cloves
250g/9oz peppers (green or red, best half and half)
200g/7oz aubergine (eggplant)
250g/9oz courgettes (optional)
6 tablespoons of olive oil
½ teaspoon of salt
1 teaspoon of sugar
150g/5oz diced cured *serrano* ham (optional)

If you want, beforehand you can briefly boil the tomatoes to peel them. Then wash and chop the vegetables, removing the seeds from the peppers. Pour the oil into a deep frying pan or pot (traditionally cooked in a clay pot) and heat over the fire. Put in the onion, adding the garlic and peppers shortly after. When they seem soft, add the courgettes (if using) and aubergines (eggplants) and stir-fry the mixture over a low flame. Add ham cubes if you like.

After five minutes, add the tomatoes and mix them well, mashing them as they soften. Add salt and sugar, and let it cook for 15–20 minutes over a low flame. If you like, you can fry one or two eggs per person in a small frying pan with plenty of oil over a high flame.

Pisto is usually served in individual clay pots (like that of individual lasagne servings, but any medium-sized dish will do) with the fried eggs on top, sunny side up. Spaniards always eat this with bread. It is delightful to dip it ('*mojar el pan*') in the fried egg yolks.

POLLO AL CHILINDRÓN

FRIED CHICKEN WITH HAM AND RED PEPPERS

SERVES FOUR

This is Spain's most popular fried chicken dish, named after a card game. It might seem extra trouble grilling the peppers, but it fits in nicely with the frying time. Cooked like this they are a basic Spanish ingredient, sweet and juicy, and make a lovely puréed sauce.

2 red peppers
2 tablespoons olive oil
1 onion, peeled and finely chopped

salt, pepper and paprika
4 chicken quarters
l00g/4oz raw *serrano* ham,
  cubed
2 garlic cloves, skinned and finely
  chopped
1 tomato, skinned and seeded

Heat the grill to high with the peppers on the rack. Grill them for 20 minutes or so, turning the peppers a quarter of the way over every 5 minutes. The skins will blacken. Place the hot peppers in a plastic bag and leave until they are cool enough to handle – about 10 minutes – when the skins will come off easily. Peel off the skins on a plate, saving the juices. Split the peppers open and scoop out the seeds, discard these and the stalks.

Meanwhile, heat the oil in a flame-proof casserole and fry the onion slowly until soft. Rub salt, pepper and paprika into the chicken. Push the onion to the side of the pan and add the chicken pieces, frying them for about 15 minutes on each side, until rosy and golden. About five minutes before they are ready, add the ham and garlic.

Chop the peppers on a plate, then mash with a fork. Chop the tomato flesh with it and add both to the spaces in the pan. Stir, cover, turn down the heat and cook for 10 minutes. Check the seasoning of the sauce and serve. New potatoes go well.

Fresh red chillies add a kick.

GAMBAS PIL-PIL
SIZZLING HOT PRAWNS

SERVES FOUR

Everyone loves these, but you must adjust the amount of chilli according to your preference. A whole fresh chilli, dried chillies or a tiny amount of cayenne or paprika can be used.

8–12 tablespoons olive oil
350g/12oz raw prawns in the shell
1 fresh chilli, or 2 dried chillies, or ¼
  teaspoon cayenne, or 1 teaspoon
  paprika
2 garlic cloves, skinned and chopped
salt

Heat the oven to high for butane gas (220°C, 425°F, gas mark 7 at home). Pour two or three tablespoons of oil

An essential ingredient in pollo al ajillo.

each – Spaniards like more – into four individual ovenproof dishes (*cazuelitas*) and heat them in the oven.

Meanwhile, peel the prawns. If you are using fresh chilli, remove the stalk and seeds, then slice into fine rings. Deseed dried chillies and crush into tiny pieces. Distribute the garlic in the oil and add the fresh or dried chilli. Divide the prawns between the dishes and sprinkle with the salt (and cayenne or paprika if using), then stir in the oil.

Return to the oven for five minutes until the dish is really hot. Serve with cocktail sticks for picking up the prawns and plenty of good bread for mopping up the juices.

POLLO AL AJILLO A LA PARRILLA
BARBECUED OR GRILLED
GARLIC CHICKEN

SERVES FOUR

Spanish chickens taste as they are meant to, and this is an easy, but classic, way to eat them. Fish such as besugo *(one for two), pretty pink* salmonetes *(one each), or about four* sardinas *per person can be cooked in the same way, adjusting times.*

1 chicken, cut into 4 serving pieces and backbone removed, or 8 thigh portions, or 4 legs
6 garlic cloves, skinned and finely chopped
2 teaspoons salt
1 teaspoon dried thyme (optional)
4 tablespoons olive oil
2 tablespoons lemon juice
thin strip of lemon zest, finely chopped
freshly ground black pepper

It is easier to cook chicken breasts if the two end wing joints are removed, leaving only one. Remove excess skin and prick the thick parts of the flesh with a fork, then put the chicken in a shallow dish. Chop the garlic, then heap it up and cover with the salt.

With the flat side of a table knife, crush the garlic into the salt to make a paste. Put it in a cup and add the thyme, oil, and lemon juice and lemon zest.

Spoon this over the chicken, peppering it and turning the pieces several times. Leave to one side.

Light the barbecue, then let the flames die down to cook. Or heat the grill to high. Cook the chicken, turning it several times for about 15 minutes on each side, dribbling or brushing with the marinade.

Note. A warning! Do not put the cooked chicken back into the unwashed marinade dish, to serve.

SOLOMILLO DE TERNERA A LA PIMIENTE VERDE
VEAL WITH GREEN PEPPER SAUCE

You'll need peppers in the chuletas recipe.

SERVES FOUR

Green pepper is the raw grain of black pepper so in this recipe we're not talking about the vegetable of the same name. It is used to produce Spain's famous green pepper sauce, which is a tasty way to serve meat dishes. Veal sirloin in green sauce is one of the best.

4 portions of veal sirloin
25g/1oz freshly ground green pepper
50g/2oz shallot bulbs
2 tablespoons of olive oil
25g/1oz margarine
1 small glass of brandy
200ml/7fl oz cooking cream
salt

Heat a saucepan, add the oil and margarine to it, then cook the sirloin, sprinkling half of the ground green pepper and shallots on top. After a few minutes, flip the steaks over and repeat.

When they seem done, withdraw the meat and add brandy and cream to the sauce. Let it simmer and reduce to half its volume.

Next, replace the steaks and add the salt. Cook for a few minutes to let the flavours blend. At this stage you can also add some boiled potatoes to the pan.

CHULETAS DE CERDO CON ALCAPARRAS Y PIMIENTO

PORK CHOPS WITH CAPERS AND PEPPERS

SERVES FOUR

Spain produces more capers than any other country. When pickled they have just the acidity to balance fried food. This mixture is good, too, with fried fish.

2 tablespoons olive oil
1 small onion, peeled and chopped
1 green pepper, destalked, seeded and
chopped
1 red pepper, destalked, seeded and
chopped
1 garlic clove, skinned and finely
chopped
4 pork chops
1 teaspoon paprika
salt and pepper
2 tablespoons pickled capers

Heat the oil in a frying pan large enough to take the chops and fry the onion gently for 10 minutes. Add the chopped peppers and garlic and fry, stirring occasionally, until the onions are soft – about another 10 minutes.

Next, sprinkle the chops with paprika – standard practice in Spain – and the salt and pepper. Fry in the pan, pushing the vegetable mixture to the sides, or piling it on top of the chops, until these are well-cooked on both sides. Roughly chop the capers and stir into the peppers, then heat through.

CERDO CON GUISANTES Y CHAMPIÑONES EN JEREZ

PORK WITH PEAS AND MUSHROOMS IN SHERRY SAUCE

SERVES FOUR

This is an easy dish for spring or early summer. Boned pork loin is widely available and makes two neat slices each. Veal is good, too, but it is more expensive; ask for filetitos, which are tiny escalopes. Fino in Spain also comes from Montilla, and so is not a true sherry, but it is much-used in cooking.

3–4 tablespoons olive oil
2 tablespoons chopped onion
salt and pepper
600g/1¼lb boneless pork loin, sliced
into 8 escalopes
2 garlic cloves, skinned and chopped
250g/9oz button mushrooms, sliced
2 tablespoons flour
175ml/6fl oz Fino or dry sherry
1.5kg/3lb peas in the pod, shelled
about 175ml/6fl oz stock, made with
a cube

Heat 3 tablespoons of oil in a flameproof casserole and put in the onion. Cook slowly until soft, then push the onion to the sides of the pan. Salt and pepper the pork slices and fry these over a high heat until browned on both sides. Remove to a plate.

Add more oil, if needed, and the garlic and mushrooms. Cook more slowly, stirring occasionally until they soften. Sprinkle with the flour and stir this in. Add the Fino and bring gently to the boil. Return the meat to the pan, stirring it well, then add the peas. Pour in just enough stock to cover. Bring to the boil and simmer for 20 minutes, covered, until both the meat and peas are done.

Note. This is really a dish to show off fresh peas. However, frozen peas can be used; cook for 10 minutes only. Use brown (chestnut) mushrooms if you can get them.

SORBETE DE LIMÓN
LEMON SORBET

SERVES FOUR

When it is so hot that all you want to do is sit in the shade and eat ice-cream, this is the freshest and most delicious ice of all. In restaurants, it is served spooned back into the lemon shells.

3–4 lemons
200g/7oz sugar
500ml/17fl oz water
2 large egg whites

Take strips of zest from the lemons with a potato peeler and put them in a saucepan with the sugar and water. Boil for five minutes without stirring. Cool and strain. Squeeze the lemon juice and add to the mixture.

Turn the lemon liquid into a freezer-proof container and freeze for about two hours until slushy. Beat with a fork, then freeze again for about 30 minutes. Remove from the freezer and beat again. Whisk the egg whites until soft peaks form and fold into the ice. Freeze again for about an hour.

Note. At home – or if you are lucky enough to have an electric mixer on holiday – leave the ice until almost stiff. Then put it in the mixer and whisk it. Add the whisked egg whites in large dollops. This is whisked into the ice, which will go almost white. You can eat the sorbet immediately or refreeze it.

Spain's climate is perfect for juicy lemons.

It's easy to make your own sangria.

SANGRÍA
CHILLED RED WINE AND
CITRUS FRUIT PUNCH

SERVES FOUR

Some sangrías *contain brandy, but
many people prefer lighter versions. In
the south the red wines are very high
in alcohol – lethal when it's sunny! This
sangría is quite sweet, the way the
Spanish like it. If you use soda water
instead of fizzy lemon, stir in 2 tablespoons of caster sugar first.*

8–10 ice cubes
4 oranges
2 lemons
**½ cinnamon stick or 1 teaspoon ground
    cinnamon**
1 litre bottle red wine, well chilled
750ml/I ¼ pints fizzy lemonade, chilled

Put the ice cubes into a jug that will hold
at least 2 litres/3½ pints. Take a thin strip
of zest from one orange and one lemon.
Add these, with the cinnamon, to the
jug. Squeeze and add all the juice, with
the red wine. Chill in the refrigerator
for a couple of hours. Top up with fizzy
lemonade just before serving.

LIMONADA FRESCA
LEMONADE

*Small children can make this
themselves. It is full of vitamin C and a
fraction of the price of drinks you buy in
the supermarket. One particular brand
of flower honey in Spain is sold with a
snap-shut pourer, which is ideal for this.
For one glass, squeeze the juice from a
lemon and pour into a tall glass with two
or three ice cubes. Add 1 tablespoon
sugar or honey, then top up with cold
water. Stir and drink.*

Use only the freshest lemons in lemonade.

Practical Information

Learning the basic Spanish phrases will help you to shop with confidence at the market.

Essentials for Travellers

SELF CATERING

Your Spanish kitchen is unlikely to contain a teapot or kettle, pepper mill or egg cups, and it is worth taking your favourite knife with you (but remember to check it in with your luggage if flying). The pans will be different shapes from those at home, so it may be easier to cook the Spanish way rather than trying to reproduce recipes from home without the proper equipment. Investigate your cooking facilities before you start shopping. The tops of Spanish stoves are often very small, limiting you to two pans. Ovens are small, too – and the butane gas type, which is common, has no regulator, only high and low settings, though many ovens nowadays are electric. Many Spaniards cook on the barbecue outside; this is both easy and fun. Instant coffee is very expensive in Spain, but supermarkets stock most standard commodities.

SAFE WATER

Drinking fountains are marked *agua potable*. In general, places with mountains nearby (such as Madrid) have nice-tasting tap water, but coastal areas, like Barcelona and Cádiz, generally do not. If you suspect the water, avoid eating lettuce washed in it.

MINOR ILLNESSES

For upset tummies, induced by eating and drinking, kaolin tablets will help. For infections from bugs in water or food, Lomotil or Primperan are both effective. For sunstroke, Spanish chemists (*farmacía*) stock the usual range of painkillers and aspirins.

CURRENCY

The euro is the official currency of Spain, introduced in January 2002. Euro bank notes are in denominations of 5, 10, 20, 50, 100, 200 and 500 euros, and coins come in 1, 2, 5, 10, 20 and 50 cents and 1 and 2 euros.

Euro traveller's cheques are widely accepted, as are all major credit cards.

TIGHT BUDGET

You will be agreeably surprised at the cost of food and drink in Spain – from the price of gin to the cost of eating out. In the humbler places, about €6 to €9 will buy you a three-course meal with wine. Bars everywhere supply hot food – and a *ración* is enough for a main course. Much the same dishes are offered in restaurants of different categories. It makes financial sense, therefore, not to eat in cafés with a view – even if you choose to drink there. They are always more expensive.

Bottled table wine (the house choice) is always cheaper than branded bottles. Drink it with mineral water – though many Spaniards cheerfully use *La Casera* (a sugary, fizzy drink, similar to 7 Up). Water is usually good and a jug of water with ice (*con hielo*) will cost nothing. At home, teach children to make drinks with real lemons (see recipe, page 146): cheaper and nicer than bought drinks. Every eating establishment is obliged by law to offer a three-course meal with bread and wine for a set price, at lunchtime called the *menú del día* – these are often very good value.

Eat what others are eating, such as the *plato del día* (dish of the day). Bean or vegetable dishes come as a course before the meat and can be very filling – enough for a whole meal in many cases. They can also be paired with soup or eggs, though these are all really alternatives. Adapt to local food, rather than looking for what you eat at home. *Tortillas* are very filling and come with lots of variations. Fish and shellfish are excellent, especially on the coast. Fresh grilled sardines are cheaper than other fish and very good. There's always a wide range of meat options on the menu. Beef is usually a better choice in the northwest; lamb and pork in Castilla; and pork in the south.

You can also take advantage of the large Spanish portions to share salads or a starter. Fruit is cheaper than dessert and normally two fruits are brought. Out shopping, street markets are weekly in most towns and villages, and these are useful, especially if you are on holiday for more than a week.

Finally, make the most of your holiday to eat luxuries that are expensive at home. In Spain you can afford to buy avocados by the kilo, and strawberries and artichokes in season cost little. Gorge on oranges and wonderful tomatoes. These really are a bargain!

SPECIAL EVENTS

Spanish festivals are enormous fun but they disrupt shopping and banks, and restaurants may be closed just before them, and are booked up during them. The Spanish Tourist Office publishes a brochure every year, called the Calendar of Celebrations, with the dates of the main ones. However, almost every village celebrates its own saint's day.

The two public holidays that catch tourists unawares are Corpus Christi, the second Thursday after Whit Sunday, and Assumption, which is 15 August. If the latter falls on a Thursday, shops may be shut for four days. Since Saturday is a working day in Spain for many, a Tuesday or Friday holiday is usually added to the weekend. Also many shops shut in August for a month's holiday.

Little cakes are the universal festival foods, but sadly few are of any distinction. You will, however, find exceptional roasts on festival menus – suckling pig and in particular baby lamb and kid at Easter – as well as pies called *panadés* in Mallorca.

San José on 19 March is celebrated in Valencia with the Fallas huge model sculpture contest – all except one will be ritually burnt on *mascaletá* night. Madrid celebrates with *buñuelos*, while Lent and Good Friday brings out a host of *balcalao* dishes. San Jorge (St-George's day) falls on 23 April (the tradition is to give roses to women and books to men), and many places in Valencia and Alicante, and Alcoy, celebrate Spanish victory over the Moors with a simple rice and bean dish, *moros y cristianos*.

Madrid celebrates its patron, San Isidore, around 15 May with *buñuelos* and a fortnight-long festival. The week around 15 May has banks closing at noon instead of 2pm. Corpus Christi, on the second Thursday after Whitsun, is marked by processions in Toledo and Sitges, near Barcelona.

San Juan on 22 June is celebrated with bonfires and feasting, particularly in Alicante, while Pamplona-Irunea toasts San Fermin on 6–14 July with bullrunning. Spain's National Day is 25 July, the Santiago Apóstal (St-James), celebrated particularly in Valencia and, of course, in Santiago de Compostela, where *tarta de santiago* is eaten.

Asunción on 15 August means Virgen de la Paloma in Madrid, with 15-day-long street festivals downtown, and village festivals all over the south, with processions, flamenco and *torrón* stalls. The biggest festival for San Mateo and America Day on 19 September is in Oviedo. This date is also the focus for the grape harvest festivals, which happen before picking in all the major wine-making places. In Logroño, trestle tables are set up in the streets. Here baby lamb chops are grilled over vine prunings (*sarmiento*) and served with lots of wine!

The Pilar festival, on 12 October in Zaragoza, is one of Spain's biggest, celebrating the Virgin. It is also Columbus Day. Around the same time, in mid-October, saffron is harvested in New Castile, with a celebration choosing a saffron queen.

On 1 November, *Todos Los Santos*, the only shops open are pastry shops selling *huesos de santo*, or *panellets* in Catalunya. The weeks before Christmas see *turrón*, *polvorones* and *figuritas de mazapán*. *Roscon de reyes* (yeast ring cake) is sold on Twelfth Night and 6 January (Three Kings' Day, which is when Spanish children get their presents).

CUSTOMS

YES

From another EU country for personal use (guidelines):

3,200 cigarettes, 200 cigars, 3kg of tobacco

10 litres of spirits (over 22%)

20 litres of aperitifs

90 litres of wine, of which 60 litres can be sparkling wine

110 litres of beer

From a non-EU country for your personal use, the allowances are:

200 cigarettes OR 50 cigars OR 250 grams of tobacco

1 litre of spirits (over 22%) OR 2 litres of intermediary products (eg sherry) and sparkling wine

2 litres of still wine

50 grams of perfume

0.25 litres of eau de toilette

The value limit for goods is 175 euros.

Travellers under 17 years of age are not entitled to the tobacco and alcohol allowances.

NO

Drugs, firearms, ammunition, offensive weapons, obscene material, unlicensed animals.

Useful Words and Phrases

PRONUNCIATION

■ Pronounce every letter, whatever its position in the word, eg leche (*lEh-che*). Exceptionally, 'h' is always silent, as is 'u' in 'que' and 'qui'.

■ Accentuating the correct syllable is very important in Spanish. To help you, stressed vowels are in capitals in the imitated pronunciation, eg vino blanco (*bEE-no blAn-co*).

■ Spanish 'a' is pronounced like 'a' in 'father', but shorter; (and **not** as in 'hat' or 'hate') eg hasta mañana (*As-ta ma-nyA-na*).

■ Spanish 'e' is pronounced like 'e' in best or 'a' in 'Mary'; (and **not** as in 'he') eg bien (*byEn*), medio (*mEh-dyo*). 'er' is pronounced like Scottish 'er' in 'person', or like 'air' in English, eg supermercado (*soo-per-mer-kA-do*).

■ Spanish 'I' is pronounced like 'ee' in 'sheep', but shorter (and **not** as in 'right'). In the imitated pronunciation it is written as 'EE' if stressed, otherwise as 'I'. 'I' before another vowel is short 'guide', written as 'y' in the imitated pronunciation, eg si (*sEE*), pimienta (*pi-myEn-ta*).

■ Spanish 'o' is pronounced like 'o' in 'hot' (**not** as in 'low'), eg sopa (*sO-pa*).

■ Spanish 'u' is always pronounced as 'u' in pudding, eg fruta (*frOO-ta*).

■ Spanish 'r' is always strongly 'rolled', especially 'rr'. Children imitating an electric buzzer with the tip of their tongue come closer to the correct sound.

■ Spanish 'z' and 'c' before 'e' and 'I' are pronounced like 'th' in 'thing', eg cien (*thyEn*), zumo (*thOO-mo*). In some parts of Spain and Latin America this sound is pronounced like an 's'.

■ Spanish 'j' and 'g' before an 'e' or an 'I' resemble the 'ch' in Scottish 'loch'. In the imitated pronunciation it is shown as a capital H, eg naranja (*na-rAn-Ha*) and softer in the south of Spain.

■ 'll' is pronouncd like 'lli' in 'million', in some parts of Spain and Latin America like 'y' in 'yes', eg paella (*pa-El-lya*).

■ 's' is always pronounced as in 'sing' (**not** as in 'rose').

■ Spanish 'v' is often heard as a 'b', 'd' as a 'th'.

HELPFUL PHRASES

Could you say it again? ¿Puede volver a repetir? *pwEh-de vol-vEr a re-pe-tEEr*

I don't understand No comprendo *no kom-prEn-do*

Please speak more slowly ¿Puede hablar más despacio? *pwEh-de a-blAr mAs des-pA-thyo*

Please write it down Por favor, escríbalo *por fa-vOr es-krEE-ba-lo*

Do you speak English? ¿Habla inglés? *A-bla in-glEs*

Where are you from? ¿De dónde es usted? *deh dOhndeh Ehs oostEhdh*

Is there anyone who speaks...? ¿Hay alguien que hable...? *ay Ahlgyehn keh Ahbleh...*

Where's the main street? ¿Dónde esta la calle major? *DOn-deh ehstAH lah cAHyeh mahyOhr*

QUESTIONS AND ANSWERS

What...? ¿Qué...? *kEh*

Why...? ¿Por qué...? *por kEh*

Which (pl)...? ¿Cuál (es)...? *kwAl es*

How...? ¿Cómo...? *KO-mo*

How long...? ¿Cuánto tiempo...? *kwAn-to tyEm-po*

How much (how many)...? ¿Cuánto (a, os, as)...? *kwAn-to (a, os, as)*

When...? ¿Cuándo? *kwAhndoh*

I don't know No lo sé *noh loh sEh*

TIME

When does the shop shut? ¿Cuándo se cierra la tienda? *kwAn-do se thiEr-ra la tyEn-da*

What time is it? ¿Qué hora es? *kEh Ohrah Ehs*

DIFFICULTIES

Go away! Come back! !Váyase !Vuelva! *vAh-ya-se, vwEl-va*

Excuse me (to get past) Perdóne *per-dO-ne*

I am sorry Lo siento *lo syEn-to*

Can you help me? ¿Puede ayudarme? *pwEh-de a-yoo-dAr-rne*

Does it bother you (pl) if (I smoke)? ¿Les molesta, si (fumo)? *les mo-lEs-ta see fOO-mo*

It does'nt matter No importa *no im-pOr-ta*

Where are the toilets? ¿Estén dónde los servicios? *dOn-de es-tAn los ser-vEE-thios*

Could I use your phone? ¿Podria llamar por teléfono? *pohdrEEah lyahmAhr pohr tehlEhfohnoh*

They are over there Están allí *es-tAn ah-lyEE*

I (we) would like... Quisiera (quisieramos)... *ki-syEh-ra, ki-sye-rA-mos*

What is this, that? ¿Qué es esto(a), ese(a)? *kEh es Es-to(a), Eh-se(a)*

GREETINGS

Yes (no) Sí (no) *sEE (nO)*

Please Por favor *por fa-vOr*

Thank you (very much) (Muchas) gracias *mOO-chas grA-thias*

Hello (goodbye) Hola (adiós) *O-la, a-dyOs*

How are you? ¿Cómo está? *kO-mo es-tA*

Well, and you? Muy bien ¿Y usted (tú)? *mOOy byEn, EE oo-ste Eth, (too)*

My name is ... Me llamo.. *me lyA-mo*

Delighted (to meet you) Encantado(a) *en-kan-tA-do(a)*

This is my wife (husband) Esta(e) es mi mujer (marido) *Es-ta(e) es mi moo-HEr (ma-rEE-do)*

Good morning Buenos días *bwEh-nos dEE-as*

Good evening (goodnight) Buenas tardes (noches) *bwEh-nas tAr-des (nO-ches)*

Tomorrow (in the morning) Mañana (por la mañana) *ma-nyA-na (por la ma-nyA-na)*

Till next time (see you later) Hasta la vista (luego) *As-ta la vEE-sta (lwEh-go)*

Greetings Saludos *sa-luh-dohs*

Where is (are)...? ¿Dónde está (están)...? *dOn-de es-tA (es-tAn)*

Have a good trip Buen viaje *bwEhn byAhheh*

NUMERALS

1	uno (una)	*OO-no, OO-na*
2	dos	*dOs*
3	tres	*trEhs*
4	cuatro	*kwA-tro*
5	cinco	*thEEn-ko*
6	seis	*sEh-is*
7	siete	*syEh-te*
8	ocho	*O-cho*
9	nueve	*nwEh-ve*
10	diez	*dyEth*
11	once	*On-the*
12	doce	*dO-the*
15	quince	*kEEn-the*
20	veinte	*vEh-in-te*
25	veinticinco	*veh-in-ti-thEEn-ko*
30	treinta	*trEh-in-ta*
40	cuarenta	*kwa-rEn-ta*
50	cincuenta	*thin-kwEnta*
60	sesenta	*se-sEn-ta*
70	setenta	*se-tEn-ta*
80	ochenta	*o-chEn-ta*
90	noventa	*no-vEn-ta*
100	cien (ciento)	*thyEn (thyEn-to)*
150	ciento cincuenta	*thyEn-to thin-kwEnta*
200	doscientos(as)	*dos-thyEn-tos(as)*
300	trescientos(as)	*tres-thyEn-tos(as)*
400	cuatrocientos(as)	*kwa-tro-thyEn-tos(as)*
500	quinientos(as)	*ki-nYen-tos(as)*
600	seiscientos(as)	*sEh-is-thyEn-tos(as)*
700	setecientos(as)	*se-te-thyEn-tos(as)*
800	ochocientos(as)	*o-cho-thyEn-tos(as)*
900	novecientos(as)	*no-ve-thyEn-tos(as)*
1000	mil	*mEEl*

GOING SHOPPING

Is there a supermarket near here?
¿Hay un supermercado por aquí?
A-ee oon soo-per-mer-kA-do por a-Kee

What day is the market? ¿Qué días hay
mercado? *ke dEE-as a-ee mer-kA-do*

I want (need) to buy... Quiero comprar
kyEh-ro kom-prAr...

I would like... Quisiera... *ki-syEh-ra*

Do you have? ¿Tiene...? *tyEh-ne*

Some (a little)... Un poco de...
oon pO-ko de

Bigger, smaller Más grande, más
pequeño *mas grAn-de, mas pe-kEh-nyo*

Can I help myself? ¿Puedo servirme?
pwEh-do ser-vEEr-me

What does it cost? ¿Cuánto es?
kwAn-to Es

Anything else? ¿Algo más? *Al-go mas*

That's it (no more) Nada más *NA-da mAs*

This is the cheapest Es el (la) más barato
(a) *es el (la) mAs ba-rA-to (a)*

Go to the checkout (till) Pase por caja
pA-se por kA-Ha

Where are the drinks? ¿Dónde están las
bebidas? *dOn-de-es-tAn las be-bEE-das*

Do you have cold meats? ¿Tiene
fiambres? *tyEh-ne fyAm-bres*

I want to buy slices Quisiera comprar
lonchas *ki-syEh-ra kom-prAr lOn-chahs*

I want fish for soup Quiero pescados
para sopa *kyEh-ro pes-kA-dos pa-ra sO-pa*

Please clean them Límpielos, por favor
lEEm-pyeh-los por fa-vOr

Without heads and filleted
Sin cabezas, y en filetes
sin ka-bEh-thas, ee en fi-lEh-tes

MEALS

We would like something to eat
Quisiéramos algo para comer
Ki-syE-ra-mos Al-go pa-ra ko-mEr

Lunch Ealmuerzo *eal-mwEr-tho*

Meal, usually lunch La comida
la ko-rnEE-da

Aperitifs (and snacks in general)
Aperitivos *a-pe-ri-tEE-vos*

Bar snacks Tapas *tA-pas*

Dinner, supper La cena *la thEh-na*

Buffet or 'open table' La mesa franca,
buffet la *mEh-sa frAn-ka, boo-fEt*

WEIGHTS AND MEASURES

1kg/generous 2lb Un kilo *oon kEE-lo*

½kg/1lb Medio kilo *Meh-dyo kEE-lo*

¼kg/½lb Un cuarto kilo
oon kwAr-to kEE-lo

100g/¼lb Cien gramos *tyEn grA-mos*

1l/1¾ pint milk Un litro de leche oon
lEE-tro de lEh-che

Half Medio *mEh-dyo*

Twice that Doble *dOh-ble*

A dozen Una docena *oo-na do-thEh-na*

MONEY

I want to change some travellers' cheques Quisiera cambiar los cheques de viaje
ki-sYEh-ra kam-byAr los chE-kes de vyA-he

Can I pay with this credit card? ¿Se suede pagar con esta tarjeta de crédito?
se pwEh-de pa-gAr kon Es-ta tar-HEh-ta de krE-di-to

AT THE RESTAURANT

What time do you serve meals? ¿A qué hora se come? *a kEh O-ra se kO-me*

I want to reserve a table for four (six) people Quiero reservar una mesa para cuatro (seis) personas
kyEh-ro re-ser-vAr oo-na MEh-sa para kwA – tro (sEh-is) per-sO-nas

I prefer non-smoking Prefiero no fumadores *pre-fyEh-ro no foo-ma-dO-res*

The menu, please La carta, por favor
la kAr-ta por fa-vOr

A bottle of red wine Una botella de vino tinto *Oona bo-tEl-lya de bEE-no tEEn-to*

We would like coffee Quisieramos tomar café *ki-syE-ra-mos to-mAR ka fEh*

May I have the bill, please? La cuenta, por favor *la kwEn-ta por fa-vOr*

Is service included?
¿El servicio está incluido?
eser-vEE-thyo es-tA in-kloo-EE-do

Do you accept this credit card (travelles' cheques)? ¿Acepta usted esta tarjeta de crédito (cheques de viaje)? *a-thEp-ta oo-stEth es-ta tar-HEh-ta de krEh-di-to (chEh-kes de vyA-he)*

We enjoyed it, thank you
Nos ha gustado, muchas gracias
nOs a goo-stA-do mOO-chas grA-thias

SPECIAL REQUIREMENTS

Do you have vegetarian dishes?
¿Tiene platos vegetarianos?
tyEh-ne plA-tos ve-He-ta-ryA-nos

Is there any meat in it? ¿Hay carne en este plato? *A-ee kAr-ne en Es-te plA-to*

I cannot eat flour (milk, sugar) No puedo comer harina (leche, azúcar)
no pwEh-do ko-mEr a-rEE-na, (lEh-che, a-thOO-kar)

I am diabetic Soy diabético(a)
sOy dya-bEh-ti-ko(a)

I am allergic to mussels, (shellfish) Soy alérgico(a) a los mejillones (mariscos)
sOy a-lEr-Hi-ko a los me-Hil-lyO-nes (ma-rEE-skos)

Is it very spicy (hot)? ¿Es picante?
es pi-kAn-ter

Another plate, please Otro Plato por favor *O-tro plA-to por fa-vOr*

Some teaspoons Unas cucharillas
OO-nas koo-cha-rEEl-lyas

Have you got a high chair, please?
¿Tiene una silla alta, por favor?
tyeh-ne OO-na sEEl-lya Al-ta por favor

Please could you warm up the baby's bottle? ¿Puede calentar ebiberón de bebé? *pwEh-de ka-len-tAr ebi-be-rOn debe-bEh*

Conversion Tables

NOTES ON USING THE RECIPES

Weights and measures are written in metric and imperial. Follow only one set of measures as they are not interchangeable.

FLUID CONVERSIONS

125ml/4fl oz	500ml/17fl oz
150ml/¼ pint (5fl oz)	600ml/1 pint (20fl oz)
175ml/6fl oz	750ml/1¼ pints
200ml/7fl oz	1 litre/1¾ pints
300ml/½ pint (10fl oz)	2 litres/3½ pints

WEIGHT CONVERSIONS

50g/2oz	175g/6oz	700g/1½lb
75g/3oz	250g/9oz	1kg/2lb
100g/4oz	350g/12oz	1.5kg/3lb
150g/5oz	500g/1lb	2kg/4lb

SPOON MEASURES

Spoon measures refer to the standard measuring spoons and all quantities are level unless otherwise stated. Do not use table cutlery and serving spoons as their capacity varies.

½ teaspoon – 2.5ml

1 teaspoon – 5ml

1 tablespoon – 15ml (3 teaspoons)

ABBREVIATIONS

Metric	Imperial
g – gram or gramme	oz – ounce
kg – kilogram	lb – pound
ml – millilitre	fl oz – fluid oz

OVEN TEMPERATURES

The following settings are used in the recipes in this book, providing centigrade, Fahrenheit and gas settings. However, cooking facilities in holiday accommodation may be limited or oven settings may be different or unreliable, so watch dishes carefully when baking in an unfamiliar appliance.

110°C	225°F	gas ¼
120°C	250°F	gas ½
140°C	275°F	gas 1
150°C	300°F	gas 2
160°C	325°F	gas 3
180°C	350°F	gas 4
190°C	375°F	gas 5
200°C	400°F	gas 6
220°C	425°F	gas 7
230°C	450°F	gas 8
240°C	475°F	gas 9

AMERICAN MEASURES AND TERMS

Liquids:

	Imperial	American
	5fl oz	²/₃ cup
	8fl oz	1 cup
	10fl oz	1¼ cups
	16fl oz	2 cups
	20fl oz (1 pint)	2½ cups

Solids: Whole pounds and fractions of a pound are used for some ingredients, such as butter, vegetables and meat. Cup measures are used for storecupboard foods, such as flour, sugar and rice. Butter is also measured by sticks.

	Imperial	American
Butter	8oz	1 cup (2 sticks)
Cheese, grated, hard	4oz	1 cup
Flour	4oz	1 cup
Haricot beans, dried	6oz	1 cup
Mushrooms, sliced	8oz	2½ cups
Olives, whole	4oz	1 cup
Parmesan, grated	1oz	3 tablespoons, 2oz/¹/₃ cup
Peas, shelled	4oz	1 cup
Raisins	6oz	1 cup
Rice (uncooked)	8oz	1 cup

Acknowledgements

1 AA/M Chaplow; 5 AA/C Sawyer; 6 AA/M Jourdan; 7 AA/P Baker; 11 AA/M Jourdan; 12 AA/M Chaplow; 15 AA/M Jourdan; 16 AA/P Enticknap; 19 AA/P Enticknap; 20 AA/J A Tims; 23 AA/K Paterson; 26 AA/M Chaplow; 33 AA/M Chaplow; 36 AA/M Jourdan; 41 AA/M Chaplow; 44 AA/M Chaplow; 48 AA/C Sawyer; 55 AA/C Sawyer; 59 Bananastock; 65 AA/M Jourdan; 70 AA/P Bennett; 79 AA/C Sawyer; 83 AA/J Cowhan; 89 AA/C Sawyer; 93 AA/R Strange; 94 AA/P Enticknap; 95 AA/S Watkins; 99 AA/P Wilson; 100 AA/J Edmanson; 103 AA/M Jourdan; 105 AA/S McBride; 106 AA/M Chaplow; 109 AA/P Wilson; 110 AA/P Bennett; 115 AA/C Sawyer; 117 AA/C Sawyer; 118 AA/M Chaplow; 120 AA/S McBride; 121 AA/C Sawyer; 122 AA/J A Tims; 123 AA/P Wilson; 124 AA/M Chaplow; 125 AA/S McBride; 126 AA/P Enticknap; 130 Photodisc; 133 AA/E Meacher; 134 AA/C Sawyer; 136 AA/A Mockford & N Bonetti; 141 AA/K Paterson; 142 Stockbyte; 143 AA/C Sawyer; 145 AA/E Meacher; 146t AA/E Meacher; 146b AA/C Sawyer; 147 AA/P Enticknap